AIDS, GAYS, and the AMERICAN CATHOLIC CHURCH

▼

Richard L. Smith

Foreword by Robert N. Bellah

THE PILGRIM PRESS
Cleveland, Ohio

The Pilgrim Press, Cleveland, Ohio 44115
© 1994 by Richard L. Smith

Published 1994

Printed in the United States of America on acid-free paper

99 98 97 96 95 94   5 4 3 2 1

Library of Congress Cataloging-in-Publication Data

Smith, Richard L. (Richard Leslie), 1950–
    AIDS, gays, and the American Catholic Church / by Richard L. Smith.
        p.   cm.
    Includes bibliographical references and index.
    ISBN 0-8298-1011-0
    1. Homosexuality—Religious aspects—Catholic Church.   2. AIDS
(Disease)—Religious aspects—Catholic Church.   3. Catholic Church—
Doctrines.   I. Title.
    BX1795.H66S65   1994
    261.8'35766'08822—dc20
                                                                94-3396
                                                                CIP

AIDS, Gays, and the
American Catholic Church

For Rob

Contents

Acknowledgments

This book emerges from conversations I have been privileged to share with some extraordinary people. Professor John Coleman, S.J., of the Graduate Theological Union accompanied me through the initial drafts. I could not have asked for a better guide. John knew just when to encourage and when to challenge. His thoughtful reflections on American Catholicism helped me to clarify my convictions and put them into words.

Professor Robert N. Bellah of the University of California at Berkeley, who graciously wrote the Foreword, provided valuable comments as the text neared its final stages. His previous works, his command of the sociological tradition, and his own conviction that good societies, both civil and ecclesiastical, must find room for gays and people with AIDS have been a constant and rich inspiration to me.

Professor Clare Fisher of the Graduate Theological Union likewise provided both stimulating reflections and genuine encouragement for the project. She once more proved herself to be a uniquely creative scholar and generous teacher.

Along the way, I was fortunate to have visited with the extraordinary ministers you will meet in chapter 4. More than once, as I listened to their stories, I had the feeling that I was standing on holy ground. These women and men have accompanied persons with AIDS, their lovers, families, and friends through many a dark night. They have often done so without the applause they so richly deserve. I applaud them now, and thank them for their time and willingness to share their stories with me.

When I first began this book, several Jesuits of the Oregon Province, in whose company I spent many wonderful years, gave me much encouragement and support. I am grateful for their vote of confidence. The final product, of course, is one for which I must assume full responsibility.

I am also indebted to Richard Brown, editor of The Pilgrim Press, and to Pilgrim's competent and dedicated staff, for the very fine suggestions they have made throughout the publication process. They have been a delight to work with. Likewise, the staff of the Graduate Theological Union Library were unfailing in providing me with their kind and capable assistance during the research phase.

Finally, I am grateful to Rob Tan, my lover and best friend. His warm heart, bright smile, and willingness to believe in me have subtly shaped my own soul, and this book as well.

Foreword

The constant increase in complexity in contemporary societies creates changes that are encouraging, disheartening, and always profoundly challenging. Part of what we are living through is an effort to make a great moral advance, to overcome structures of domination that have characterized human societies for millennia. The most striking such effort is the struggle for the equality of women with men. Historically, the subordination of women to men is the most deeply entrenched of all the forms of social domination. But at the same time we are experiencing the effort to overcome domination by race, class, and sexual orientation. While the overcoming of domination in any of these respects is not imminent, it is still remarkable that contemporary society has put these issues on the agenda, has begun serious discussion of them, and has taken preliminary steps toward the elimination of these forms of domination.

While the effort to overcome domination and oppression in these various forms can only be seen as an effort toward moral advance, there are other changes in contemporary society, some of them even related to the struggle against domination, that suggest moral breakdown. The challenge to previously accepted ways of structuring the relation between dominant and subordinate groups has gone hand in hand with the challenge to normative order itself. Individual freedom, which, rightly understood, is certainly a noble cause, has been used as an argument for the abandonment of such traditional virtues as loyalty and responsibility, undermining commitment to spouse, family, friends, and community. If traditional structures were oppressive there is the temptation to abandon structures altogether, with chaotic consequences. The American gay community has certainly been caught up in this double movement of moral liberation on the one hand and anarchy on the other.

The Catholic church in America has also been caught up in this double movement, in part sanctioning the struggle against oppression and in part attempting to hold the line against anarchy. For significant reasons it has been easier for the church to take the side of those oppressed because of class (the preferential option for the poor) and race. Gender equality and equality of sexual orientation, however, raise issues that are deeply embedded in the structure of the church itself and are much more threatening to deal with.

Let's face it: sexuality and domination are scary. It has been argued that the negative attitude toward sexuality characteristic of the early Christian church, and to a considerable extent still characteristic of the church, and not only the Catholic church, derives from Christian opposition to the forms of domination in which sexuality was embedded in classical antiquity, forms of domination in both heterosexual and homosexual relations. The ideal of chastity or celibacy, then, would be related to the Christian rejection of coercion and violence in human relationships. The subordination of women in the early church, a protracted and complex process, would be seen as in part the subordination of the temptation to sexuality that women represent, and in part a return of the primordial sexual subordination of women in another form. In any case, calling into question long-standing compromise solutions to deeply disturbing problems is bound to create anxiety and defensiveness, particularly in the hierarchical structures of the church.

What makes the present situation so poignant is that the clerical hierarchy, represented in Richard Smith's book by the statements of the American bishops, is responding to the threat of normative anarchy as well as to the demand for liberation from domination. Holding the line on traditional teachings about sexuality (and gender) may seem to be essential to holding the line against antinomianism in general. What makes the situation particularly painful when it comes to the relation between the church and gays—and the church's attitude toward AIDS— is that the gay community has in many respects led the way in the antinomian crusade. It is this painful and difficult situation that Smith explores with both candor and tact.

What I take it Smith argues, and which I affirm, is that a principled rejection of gay sexuality, whether put forward by the church or any other sector of society, is morally indefensible. It has the same status today as arguments for the inferiority of women. To remain stuck in that position, as the church for the time being seems likely to do, is not only unfortunate: it makes the church collaborate in continuing forms of domination. To put it even more strongly: it makes the church collaborate in sin. But at the same time the church is under no obligation to affirm the antinomian tendencies of our culture, gay or otherwise. Rather it should undertake the difficult task of attempting to create a context of love and moral responsibility for homosexual relationships as for heterosexual ones. Just as long experience has taught the church that the effort to bring heterosexuality into a context of moral responsibility will never be more than partially successful, so we cannot expect that a new understanding of loyal and responsible homosexual relationships will not often enough be broken in practice. But, and here again I agree with Smith, creating such a persuasive ideal is what the problem is and that is where the energy of the church should be going.

Smith's careful reading of the bishops' statements on AIDS usefully elucidates the strengths and weaknesses of their position, focusing on the inadequacy of the metaphors for sexuality in the current teaching, but also emphasizing the seriousness with which the bishops take the AIDS epidemic and the nonjudgmental compassion they extend to those afflicted. But to me the greatest contribution of the book is the close attention it gives to the way in which the church through its ground-level activists is actually making itself present in the midst of suffering and death. In the ministries of care that are being carried out all across the country the lineaments of a practical Catholic ethic for gays and AIDS are being worked out. What Smith observes needs intelligent theological and ethical reflection, not simple affirmation. The virtue of this book is that it begins the task of giving just such helpful reflection. It will not do to substitute expressive individualism for unreflective moralism, and that is a real temptation in the gay community, as Smith's data show. But a genuine attention to the lived reality of gay life in contemporary America is the essential starting point for any reflection that would put it in the context of a Christian form of life.

The AIDS epidemic serves as a kind of Rorschach test for Western civilization. For a long time the Romantic strand in our culture has connected forbidden love and death. Anxieties about sexuality are enormously heightened when it is connected to a disease that ends in protracted suffering and inevitable death. It is not surprising that the reaction is often irrational: fear and anger are common on every side. Into this fraught situation Smith brings the voice of reason. He does not pretend to be disengaged. He makes it clear where his commitments lie.

But it is not his intention to find the villains and convict them. In the midst of all the irrationality he seeks a Catholic solution that will be faithful to tradition and to the lived realities of our time. The way in which he combines social scientific, ethical, and theological reflection is exemplary. May there be many who listen and continue the conversation he has begun.

ROBERT N. BELLAH
University of California at Berkeley

Introduction

Some of the signs they carried outside St. Patrick's Cathedral that New York morning in December 1989 said things like "Stop This Man," "Curb Your Dogma," and "Danger: Narrow-Minded Church Ahead." Most of the demonstrators were either abortion rights advocates or members of the AIDS Coalition to Unleash Power (ACT UP), the loosely organized but highly sophisticated activist group that had already proven itself on the American landscape as a force to be reckoned with when it came to AIDS. Organized in 1987 by Larry Kramer, the novelist and founder of New York's Gay Men's Health Crisis, ACT UP had already successfully lobbied for and won bills that would protect persons living with AIDS (PWAs) from discrimination in housing and in the workplace, forced the Food and Drug Administration to speed up the approval process for drugs used in treating AIDS, and gained a commitment from Burroughs-Wellcome Pharmaceutical Company to lower their prices for the AIDS drug known as AZT. ACT UP had gotten action. Now it was Cardinal O'Connor they were after. "Teach safe sex," they shouted, and "'Just say no' is not enough."

Events quickly escalated as the protesters moved inside the cathedral to disrupt the cardinal's mass. One activist deliberately dropped a consecrated communion wafer on the floor. Many lay down in the aisles, threw condoms in the air, chained themselves to pews, or shouted invectives at the cardinal. Forty-three activists were arrested and carried out of the cathedral; another sixty-eight were arrested in the streets.

O'Connor, the activists pointed out, had frequently opposed both women's right to abortion (he once proposed forming an order of nuns to work against the provision of abortion) and gay civil rights. (New York's Gay Rights Bill was passed in 1986 over his fierce opposition. He ousted the gay Catholic group Dignity from church premises and got an injunction against Dignity's silent protests in front of the cathedral.

1

"The clear message from O'Connor's pulpit," gay activist Douglas Crimp wrote, "is that gay people are immoral, and fagbashers have taken heed: violence against lesbians and gays has sharply increased in the past decade."[1])

While many gay and AIDS activists such as Larry Kramer applauded the protest that day at St. Patrick's, it nevertheless created no small controversy within other segments of those same communities. "If I didn't know better," wrote gay *San Francisco Chronicle* columnist Randy Shilts, "I'd swear that the AIDS protesters who have been disrupting services and vandalizing Catholic churches...were being paid by some diabolical reactionary group dedicated to discrediting the gay community."[2] Similarly, Peter Staley, a twenty-eight-year-old former bond trader and ACT UP leader, called the protests an "utter failure" and "a selfish, macho thing." By shifting the focus to issues of religious freedom, Staley argued, the church protests took the spotlight away from AIDS.[3]

Regardless of how one evaluates the wisdom of their demonstration, however, it remains a fact that ACT UP members were not the only ones concerned about the church hierarchy's recent pronouncements on AIDS. Such highly respected public officials as the then–surgeon general, Dr. C. Everett Koop,[4] and San Francisco's then–director of public health, Dr. Mervyn Silverman,[5] both of whom bore heavy public responsibility for preventing the epidemic's spread, had found themselves in significant disagreement with some aspects of the hierarchy's statement, particularly its position on safer sex education and the use of condoms.

In 1987, the American bishops, through the administrative board of the United States Catholic Conference, had issued their statement "The Many Faces of AIDS," in which they reaffirmed traditional Catholic teachings on matters sexual, yet simultaneously gave a carefully circumscribed allowance for education on safer sex, including condoms. The church, they reasoned, is only one part of a larger, pluralistic American society. Since not all Americans will agree with our sexual code, much less follow it, we have to take some responsibility for slowing the spread of the epidemic. A lesser evil, the use of condoms, may be allowed in order to prevent a worse evil, the spread of AIDS.

However, even this carefully reasoned statement was significantly revised upon the insistence of Cardinal O'Connor, with support from the Vatican and his conservative colleagues among the American episcopacy. Since, in the revisors' view, condoms were essentially a form of artificial birth control, to give even a highly qualified allowance for them would have at least three serious consequences: it would delude people into thinking that condoms made sex safer than was actually the case; it would make it easier for them to engage in promiscuous sexual behavior; it would confuse the Catholic faithful who had always been taught that artificial birth control was wrong. Indeed, several news stories around the country had already interpreted the initial AIDS statement as a softening of traditional Catholic teaching on birth control. Therefore, O'Connor and his cohorts reasoned, the only credible proposal the bishops could make for halting the spread of AIDS would be sexual abstinence and faithful monogamy. The final statement, "Called to Compassion and Responsibility," ratified by a vote of 219–4, stated clearly: "It is not condom use that is the solution to this health problem."[6] No more education on so-called safer sex. Period. The demonstration in front of St. Patrick's Cathedral took place two weeks after the bishops' second statement was released.

Political movements are rarely simple. A variety of interests converged in the demonstration at the cathedral that Sunday morning. At issue for many of the AIDS activists was the need not only to halt the spread of AIDS, but also to challenge the traditional Catholic teaching on sexuality itself. Many of the demonstrators had long since rejected the traditional Catholic sexual ethic as irrelevant, if not downright oppressive, especially for women and gay men. If the activists wanted to promote the use of condoms, it was because they not only wanted *safer* sex, but also safer *sex*.[7] For them, the condom was not only a prophylactic, but also a sign of determination, AIDS notwithstanding, to assert and enjoy the sexual freedom they had gained after many hard battles with political and religious leaders like O'Connor. Their need to prevent the transmission of the virus converged with their desire to safeguard hard-won sexual freedoms. Hence, their promotion of condoms.

If Cardinal O'Connor wanted to discourage the use of condoms, it was not only because he saw "safer sex" as a dangerous illusion that merely served to perpetuate the epidemic's spread, but also because he saw the epidemic as an opportunity to reassert the traditional Catholic sexual ethic, particularly its proscriptions against homosexual behavior and artificial birth control. Hence his opposition to condom education and his terse and unfortunate summary of the second episcopal statement that "good morality makes good medicine."

This is a book on the American Catholic construction of AIDS. It is written at a time when American Catholicism is paradoxical in many ways, and AIDS happens to be one of the issues that reflect that paradox.

On the one hand, with the help of what has been termed the "Restoration" of a pre–Vatican II ethos by Pope John Paul II, the American bishops, with Cardinal O'Connor frequently at the forefront, have reasserted traditional Catholic positions regarding women, abortion, birth control, homosexuality, and family life. This approach relies almost uniquely on magisterial authority, is methodologically deductive, and arrives at relatively fixed conclusions. No room for dialogue here. Toe the line or leave. Many American Catholics, especially Catholic women, have chosen the latter course.[8]

In this same period, however, the American Catholic hierarchy has shown great courage, clarity, and imagination in addressing the economic injustices and the proliferation of nuclear weapons that have plagued postwar America. They have done this through genuine dialogue with a cross section of the American people, Catholic and non-Catholic alike, in all levels and walks of life. A healthy facility for respectful and genuine dialogue, a willingness to listen and to learn, is evident here. This strain of the American Catholic tradition exhibits a remarkable openness to a plurality of opinions and perspectives, a flexibility in coming to terms with previously unknown realities, and an extraordinary compassion and concern for human dignity.

Two very different models of church-society relations are thus exhibited within the American church. American Catholicism today is paradoxical.

AIDS happens to be yet another occasion in which this paradox manifests itself. On the one hand, a strong social justice tradition impels the church to enter into solidarity with PWAs, to insist on their inalienable human dignity, to demand that they be given adequate treatment. This conviction about justice has been more than mere words. Catholic bishops, like Oakland's John Cummins, have led the way in fighting discrimination against PWAs. Throughout the United States, Catholic facilities have been converted to hospices for AIDS patients, and personnel and money have been put at the service of PWAs and their caregivers.[9] At the same time, the recently reinvigorated tradition on sexual morality has stigmatized a large percentage of the people who have contracted this devastating disease, especially gay men. A paradox is evident here. The American Catholic construction of AIDS is, in many ways, paradigmatic of American Catholicism itself these days.

In these pages, I want to offer a critical examination of the American Catholic construction of AIDS. Like any other meaning ascribed to AIDS, the American Catholic construction must be rigorously scrutinized to identify and ferret out elements that may be oppressive or harmful. I want to identify those oppressive and harmful elements.

Yet I also will claim that American Catholicism does indeed have abundant resources to help us make sense out of this crisis. These resources, I believe, are to be found especially within the American Catholic understanding of human community, its strong tradition of social justice, and its rich repertoire of myths, rituals, and symbols that give meaning to human suffering and death.

Drawing from the theoretical framework known as social constructionism, I am going to assume throughout this book that constructions of AIDS—whether by ACT UP or by Cardinal O'Connor—do not fall from the sky. They emerge out of various cultures from the social interactions of human beings. Social constructionism recognizes that our knowledge is not wholly objective but constructed according to the values and symbols we internalize through interaction with our culture.

There are two elements at work in this claim. First of all, it implies that we human beings are the source of the particular constructions of reality we come to take for granted as "objectively true." Second, this claim carries with it a moral imperative: We are responsible for the ways we interpret and give meaning to reality.

This responsibility demands that we critically examine our constructions of the world and of AIDS. Whose interests are being served in them? Are they adequate to all the data we have about this disease? Do they help us bring an end to this epidemic? Do they enable PWAs to live gracefully with their illness, or do they contribute to greater alienation and anxiety? Do they contribute to greater social cohesiveness as our society wrestles with AIDS, or do they contribute to social fragmentation or discrimination against PWAs and those labeled as members of "high-risk groups"?

The American Catholic construction of AIDS is a largely human construct that has emerged out of the interactions of American Catholics among themselves, their grappling with their traditions and with their larger church. As a human construct, it reflects the cultural biases and values, the power structures, the myths, symbols, rituals, and traditions that make up the fabric of Catholic life. And as a human construct, it merits careful scrutiny. What are the features of this American Catholic construction of AIDS? What voices have given it shape? Whose interests does it serve? What does it contribute to the larger American discourse on AIDS and to people affected by this disease? What are its harmful elements? These are the kinds of questions I will explore in this book.

In chapter 1, I will discuss why I believe it is so important to regard AIDS not only from a medical or political viewpoint, but from a religious one as well. Since AIDS discourse in this country has been shaped to a considerable degree by voices from within the emerging gay culture, chapter 2 will review how the church has interacted, or failed to interact, with that culture. Since the institutional Catholic church is guided by a defined hierarchy, chapter 3 will critically examine the two key statements of the American Catholic bishops on AIDS, "The Many Faces of AIDS" and "Called to Compassion and Responsibility." Since Catholic life is never fully captured in official statements but is rather lived with all its loose ends at the local level, chapter 4 will describe the efforts, experiences, and perspectives of Catholic pastoral caregivers working directly in this epidemic. In the fifth and final chapter, I will identify some of the salient implications for both the American Catholic church and the gay community, as these two communities continue their efforts to define the meaning of AIDS.

I write this book, finally, as one who considers himself lucky to have been shaped to a significant degree by both the Catholic community and the gay culture. The AIDS epidemic is a moment when these two cultures, willingly or not, are brought face-to-face by their common desire to alleviate human suffering. It is also a moment when the differences in their worldviews and ethics come into bold relief, as the ACT UP demonstration at St. Patrick's Cathedral illustrated. For someone like myself who cherishes both of these two conflicting cultures, the story of their interaction during the course of this epidemic makes a complex and fascinating grist. My hope, as I analyze their uneasy relationship during this epidemic, is a modest one: that these pages will enable people in both cultures to understand each other a little better, to work together more effectively in caring for people with AIDS and, God willing, to hasten the end of this devastating and bitter tragedy.

1 AIDS and the Religious Metaphor

AIDS is so much more than a matter of microbes. It is also a matter of human suffering.

> To discuss AIDS as suffering, we must make meanings and experience as salient to the problem of AIDS as are microbes and behavior; we need to make demoralization and threat and hope as legitimate to the public discourse on AIDS as are sexual practices, intravenous drug use, and HIV testing. If we minimize the significance of AIDS as human tragedy, we dehumanize people with AIDS as well as those engaged in the public health and clinical response to the epidemic. Ultimately, we dehumanize us all.[1]

More than simply a matter of bodily fluids, viral infections and treatment regimens, AIDS is also a complex web of conflicting emotions—rage and fear and grief, tenderness and courage. It is also a matter of human values—justice, compassion, loyalty, pride in one's identity, and love. AIDS is more than "the story of a virus," as the National Academy of Sciences once termed it.[2]

There is a fallacy that modern science has helped to propagate: that we can know things in a purely objective fashion, as though prescinding completely from our subjective interests and aspirations, our cultural biases and values. This fallacy rests on the assumption that it is possible for us to step outside of our own skin and social context and history in order to grasp reality from some imagined point outside of time and space. And though some would claim that if we could but strip ourselves of the social and cultural influences in our lives, we could then apprehend reality in its pure objectivity, this remains an impossible task. We are, at the most profound levels of our lives, all wrapped up with others in society. Our understanding of the world is profoundly shaped by culture. In other words, what we regard as real is, to a great degree, "socially constructed." Through our interaction with the people who surround us, especially the "significant others" in our lives, we come to internalize the stock of languages, myths, symbols, and values of our cultural heritage. We interpret the raw data of our experience through the cultural lens we acquire, and thereby "construct" what we come to regard as real.

Indeed, what makes us human, as anthropologist Clifford Geertz asserts, is this culturally derived ability we have to give shape and meaning to our otherwise meaningless and formless experiences.

> Undirected by cultural patterns...man's behavior would be virtually ungovernable, a mere chaos of pointless acts and exploding emotions, his experience virtually shapeless. Culture, the accumulated totality of such patterns, is not just an ornament of human existence but—the principal basis of its specificity—an essential condition of it.[3]

And culture, to paraphrase Geertz, is also an essential condition of what we have come to regard as illness. For example, not every culture, as sociologist Talcott Parsons observed, would label the same set of biological phenomena in medical terms. We Westerners, in other words, have "socially constructed" illness, including AIDS, out of the scientific categories we have developed and come to prize in our culture.

It is this theoretical framework of social constructionism that I will rely on as I discuss the American Catholic construction of AIDS. Yet, I want to use this theoretical framework carefully and avoid a mistaken cultural relativism that fails to take seriously the biomedical dimensions of AIDS. For AIDS is not purely a social construct, as some of the more relativist critics of medicine of the 1960s and 1970s might have argued. During that period, such critics stressed what, of course, is true: the physician is not somehow above cultural influence and political interest but is rather "a social actor whose mission of defining and treating disease can express and legitimate professional, class, or gender interests." As Charles Rosenberg notes, however, sociology of medicine has moved toward a post-relativist position that stands in partial contrast to aspects of the 1960s and 1970s. "[T]he weight of scholarly opinion has... shifted," Rosenberg observes, "toward an emphasis on biological factors in the understanding of disease and human behavior." AIDS has thus become "an occasion for labeling, but it is not simply an exercise in labeling."[4]

We have to acknowledge the biological dimension of AIDS: it is a deadly phenomenon within the blood and semen of many human beings; and it is capable of transmission from one human organism to another through very specific practices. For the purely pragmatic reasons of preventing the epidemic's spread, we cannot afford to overlook the biological dimensions of AIDS.

But acknowledging the biological element in itself is not enough. More than biological processes are at work in any illness, including AIDS. Let me explain by critically examining the work of Susan Sontag, who has played a major role in shaping the cultural construction of AIDS in the United States.

Sontag is perhaps one of the more articulate spokespersons insisting that we listen to the biomedical construction of AIDS. In fact, although she realizes that "one cannot think without metaphors,"[5] she largely dismisses the cultural metaphorization of disease, noting how oppressive and dysfunctional it can be to think of AIDS in such metaphorical terms as "plague," "apocalyptic catastrophe," and "war."

When she reflects back on her motives for writing her strong and poignant book *Illness as Metaphor*, Sontag writes:

> My purpose was, above all, practical. For it was my doleful observation, repeated again and again, that the metaphoric trappings that deform the experience of having cancer have very real consequences: they inhibit people from seeking treatment early enough, or from making a greater effort to get competent treatment. The metaphors and myths, I was convinced, kill. . . . I hoped to persuade terrified people who were ill to consult doctors, or to change their incompetent doctors for competent ones, who would give them proper care. To regard cancer as if it were just a disease—a very serious one, but just a disease. Not a curse, not a punishment, not an embarrassment. Without "meaning."[6]

Sontag therefore applies a hermeneutic of suspicion to the various illness and AIDS metaphors, pointing out how they fail to account for proven facts about disease, add an unnecessary and unhelpful layer of disgrace to illness, and discourage people from seeking out competent medical help. She exposes the longstanding cultural stereotypes—racist, homophobic stereotypes, often with a bias against Third World peoples—lurking within our metaphors for AIDS. She hopes to free people of the oppressive cultural overlays we put on AIDS, to present AIDS as "just a disease," and then to encourage persons living with AIDS (PWAs) to stick to proven medical facts, seek out competent medical care, and take an active role in their treatment.

Sontag is correct in taking biological data seriously. Moreover, when she exposes the oppressive and dysfunctional elements in our metaphors for illness, I believe Sontag makes an important contribution to our thinking about illness in general, and AIDS in particular. Finally, I believe she is correct to place confidence in quality medical care. Persons with AIDS do well to take seriously Sontag's encouragement to seek competent medical help and take an active role in their treatment. However, when Sontag concludes that we must discard most if not all metaphors as inevitably oppressive and dysfunctional, when she reduces AIDS to "just a disease," she then relegates us to the narrow limits of an exclusively biomedical construction of AIDS. I am not ready to suggest, as Sontag does, that we limit ourselves exclusively to this one rather narrow construction of this disease. Rather, I believe that we must take *both* the biomedical *and* the cultural constructions of AIDS seriously.

To use another disease as an example, Nancy Waxler has amply demonstrated how, in the case of leprosy, the same set of biological data are given vastly different interpretations by different cultures, and the responses to it are organized in remarkably different ways.[7] For example, in India, a society stratified according to a caste system based on the ideology of impurity and sin, lepers are shunned and isolated untouchables. In Sri Lanka, a less hierarchical society influenced by Buddhist values of tolerance and compassion, lepers bear less stigma than their counterparts in India. In Nigeria, a Muslim society, the people "exhibit little fear or disgust concerning leprosy. They do not seem to regard it with any special apprehension; it is not necessarily more unusual than any other of the great range of diseases that assail them." Finally, in the United States, a culture characterized by worldliness, activism, scientific rationality, and technical efficacy, leprosy is referred to by the medical term "Hansen's disease." Many of those who carry this disease assume the activist role of a "career patient," speaking before the Rotary Club, lobbying Congress for funds, educating the public about the nature of the disease.

Even medical facts themselves are constructed through a cultural and social process. For example, sociologists Malcolm Nicolson and Cathleen McLaughlin have noted that specifically medical constructions of multiple sclerosis have varied greatly depending on whether that disease was being examined by vascular theorists, immunologists, or neurologists. "Different observers . . . produce radically different cognitive worlds because modes of observation, and the points from which observation takes place, differ."[8] The fact that one medical construction holds sway at a given moment is as much a matter of the preference afforded to that specialty when power and money are allocated as it is a matter of that construction's scientific validity. Medical facts are not as objective as we sometimes think. This fact is significant in understanding the early constructions of what eventually came to be known as AIDS.

The early construction of AIDS was epidemiological. It focused on the population group in which the disease seemed to occur most frequently, hence the early designation of the disease as "gay-related immune deficiency" (GRID). Later, with the increased influence of virology, the medical consensus shifted. No longer was AIDS linked exclusively with gay men, but rather with certain practices that are carried out within the larger population as well. With this shift from one medical discipline to another, the construction of AIDS also shifted. Medical constructions of AIDS, far from being totally objective, have been shaped by the ever-shifting power arrangements and valuations given to various medical disciplines.[9]

Cultural bias, moreover, affects not only how we label certain biological phenomena, but also how we weigh and evaluate scientific and medical facts. This significance of cultural bias in evaluating scientific facts becomes all the more apparent when we are on the fault lines of our knowledge, in areas of grayness and uncertainty. For example, a recent study asked people for their views about the safety of irradiated food. The study found that respondents were more likely to form their opinions *not* from accurate knowledge and information presented to them, that is, not from "facts," but from the authority of institutions they trusted, specifically government and science. Respondents who were the most trusting of those institutions were more likely to consider food irradiation a safe process. "Whether respondents received a technical or non-technical communication about the food irradiation process and whether they received a detailed discussion of the major arguments for and against food irradiation had no discernible effect on their judgments."[10] The respondents formed their opinions, in other words, out of their cultural biases and values.

Similarly, with regard to AIDS, studies have indicated that those whose culture stigmatizes homosexuals are more likely to resist "facts" about the difficulty of transmitting HIV through casual contact and to favor policies that discriminate against people with AIDS.[11] Moreover, these different cultural biases seem to account for the different evaluations of the potential efficacy of any proposed solution to the epidemic. Just how effective would quarantining or national mandatory HIV testing or the promotion of "safer sex" be, anyway? "Facts" may be mustered to support any number of conflicting positions on any of these questions. In the end, one's answer is likely to be largely shaped by one's culture.

Since our American culture so frequently defines deviation from culturally accepted norms regarding health, beauty, and acceptable behavior in medical terms, this medical definition shapes the way we respond to such deviations.

Think for a moment of the difference in consequences if a person's inability to function is attributed to laziness or to mononucleosis, seizures to demon possession or epilepsy, or drinking habits to moral weakness or alcoholism. Medical diagnosis affects people's behavior, attitudes they take toward themselves, and attitudes others take toward them.[12]

Among the social consequences of adopting a medical diagnosis is that we broaden the institutional base of scientific medicine. This expanded institutionalization comes to act back upon us: we increasingly interpret our experience in medical terms and present it as a problem to be scrutinized and resolved by the medical experts.[13]

An illustration of such medicalization within American society can be seen in the 1989 petition to the Food and Drug Administration by the American Society for Plastic and Reconstructive Surgery, the major organization for plastic surgeons. That petition argued for a loosening of legal restrictions on the use of breast implants, arguing that breast enlargements are medically necessary because "these deformities [i.e., small breasts] are really a disease which in most patients results in feelings of inadequacy, lack of self-confidence, distortion of body image and a total lack of well-being due to a lack of self-perceived femininity."[14] Needless to say, cultural images of what constitutes femininity, as well as cultural values that place great weight on scientific medicine, play a significant role in interpreting small breasts as a medical disease. That medical professionals, themselves shaped by such images and values, could seriously consider defining small breasts as a "disease" testifies to the power of their profession in medicalizing our understandings of ourselves and of life.

American medicine, as Elliot Friedson observes, represents one particular culturally derived way of constructing disease: "Just like law and religion, the profession of medicine uses normative criteria to pick out what it is interested in, and . . . its work constitutes a social reality that is distinct from (and on occasion virtually independent of) physical reality."[15]

Just as we cannot ignore the biological aspects of illness, neither can we afford to be naive about its cultural constructions. This is especially true with regard to AIDS, which, insofar as it is often transmitted sexually, evokes a large inheritance of cultural metaphors for sexuality and sexual deviance.[16] This legacy of metaphors continues to frame our perceptions, including those of contemporary scientists. There is good reason, then, to take such metaphors seriously, to critically ferret them out and evaluate them, asking ourselves whether they are adequate for us as we construct our own contemporary understandings of AIDS.

Susan Sontag fails to recognize that the biomedical model, while freeing us from oppressive, religiously inspired moral judgments, nevertheless carries its own form of moral oppression. While Western medicine offers a great deal that can be helpful in understanding and responding to AIDS in a nonjudgmental way,[17] one has only to listen to the past nightmares of many women, gay men, and members of racial minority groups—stories of forced sterilizations and clitoridectomies, of castrations, electroshock and hormonal treatments, and other "reparative therapies"—to recall that the institutions of medicine are not always as free of their own moralisms and forms of oppression as Sontag seems to imply.[18] Whether consciously or not, subjectively held perceptions and values shape the way scientists approach even the most ruthlessly "objective" scientific project. True, the medical profession may not brand a person as a sinner—and this is a welcome relief. Nevertheless, it does subtly exercise its own, often oppressive, moral evaluations, as Irving Zola points out:

> For instance, while it is probably true that individuals are no longer directly condemned for being sick, it does seem that much of this condemnation is merely displaced. Though his immoral character is not demonstrated in his having a disease, it becomes evident in what he does about it. Without seeming ludicrous, if one listed the traits of people who break appointments, fail to follow treatment regimen, or even delay in seeking medical aid, one finds a long list of "personal flaws." Such people seem to be ever ignorant of the consequences of certain diseases, inaccurate as to symptomatology, unable to plan ahead or find time, burdened with shame, guilt, neurotic tendencies, haunted with traumatic medical experiences, or members of some lower status minority group—religious, ethnic, racial or socioeconomic. In short, they appear to be a sorely troubled if not disreputable group of people.[19]

Moreover, though the medical profession may not physically torture and burn those it labels as "flawed" as did earlier historical conspiracies of church and state, it does nevertheless often inflict a large amount of physical and psychological pain on its clients, not always for their health and well-being. Medical techniques, though frequently of no proven effectiveness, command considerable credibility in our culture. Witness, as but one example, the many cases of unnecessary (and expensive) surgery. "When you're in Disneyland," one physician was heard to say to a patient with AIDS, "you take all the rides."[20]

Within a purely biomedical model, AIDS is the result of a virus. It is, in Sontag's words, "just a disease," to be treated through various medical interventions. When we thus define AIDS in such exclusively biomedical terms, we ipso facto place the person with AIDS under the complete control of medical institutions and professionals. We do so, I believe, at their peril. We cannot naively assume that such a move is necessarily one of liberation from moral oppression.

There is yet another reason for taking cultural metaphors seriously. The biomedical model alone simply cannot "get at" many crucial elements of human experience. While it enables us to perceive and respond to certain aspects of the experience of AIDS, the biomedical model simultaneously prevents us from perceiving and responding to other important aspects of that experience.

One story of a man with AIDS named Robert is told by Paul Farmer and Arthur Kleinman, M.D. Robert had been admitted into the hospital with a fever, cough, and severe shortness of breath. He was diagnosed as having the opportunistic lung parasite pneumocystis and treated accordingly with the drug of choice. The treatment did not work well; in fact, Robert's fever rose and he seemed more ill than ever. After a few days of decline, Robert was found to have trismus, or a locking shut of the jaw. Because he had had a previous history of oral candidiasis ("thrush"), his trismus was thought to suggest the spread of the fungal infection back down the throat and pharynx and into the esophagus. Because he could not open his mouth, a gastroenterological treatment was considered. This treatment involved passing tubes into both ends of the gastrointestinal tract, the sort of invasive procedure that he had, on the night of his admission, declined.

Because Robert refused the treatment preferred by the medical specialists, and was therefore "not with the program," the specialists began questioning his mental competence. Perhaps he had AIDS dementia. The specialists continued trying to persuade him of the value of further diagnostic studies, but he simply stared back with a look of anger and despair.

Finally, Robert asked for a pen and paper, and, with a shaky hand, he wrote his doctors a note: "I just want to be kept clean." He died a short time later.[21]

There are some crucial issues that medical constructions of AIDS alone cannot address. Robert had available to him the most advanced medical technology to date, yet such technology could not speak to a large part of his own experience of having AIDS. True, the biomedical model serves us well in keeping track of T-cell counts, in noticing the development of lesions and pneumocystis carinii pneumonia, and in prescribing the appropriate medical treatments. However, it hides from our awareness the dimensions of grief, isolation, fear, and outrage—as well as courage and dignity and compassion—that are likely to be elements of a PWA's experience.

Nor does the biomedical model, for all of its usefulness, serve us well when we ask the inevitable questions "Why? Why me? Why this group of people? Why now?" (Sontag claims that this question is not seriously asked by many AIDS patients in the West. I disagree. She writes: "Few wonder, Why me? Most people outside of sub-Saharan Africa who have AIDS know (or think they know) how they got it."[22] But asking *why* one has a disease is not the same as asking *how* one contracted it. The latter question can indeed be handled adequately in biomedical terms; the former, a question of ultimate meaning, cannot.)

Thus, the biomedical construction of AIDS does not acknowledge or seriously address many of the elements that form the experience of one who has AIDS. It cannot adequately locate a marginal experience such as AIDS within a universe of meaning.[23] This latter task is a nonempirical one that exceeds the realm of science. It requires symbols, metaphors, and rituals; it relies on the creativity of artists, poets, musicians, novelists, dancers, and theologians.

In short, our constructions of AIDS bring into play a complex interaction between biological facts and cultural values. We must take *both* the biological data *and* the operative cultural worldviews and values seriously before we can fully understand the complex dimensions of such a human experience. To say with Sontag that metaphors are almost inevitably oppressive and detrimental is to short-circuit an indispensable part of the process through which we human beings understand and deal with illness, suffering, and death. Before we cast aside all metaphorical constructions of AIDS for the sake of the biomedical model, we would do well to consider the positive role that metaphors can play.

For although metaphors, like the biomedical model I have just critiqued, are limited, they are nevertheless necessary and useful. As constructions of reality, they can be discriminating—hiding and downplaying some aspects of our experience while revealing and highlighting others. George Lakoff and Mark Johnson use an example of a metaphor—love as a collaborative work of art:

This metaphor highlights certain aspects of love experiences, downplays others, and hides still others. In particular, it downplays those experiences that fit the LOVE IS A PHYSICAL FORCE metaphor. By "downplaying," we mean that it is consistent with, but does not focus on, experiences of love that could be reasonably described by "There is a magnetism between us," "We felt sparks," etc. Moreover, it hides those love experiences that fit the LOVE IS WAR metaphor because there is no consistent overlap possible between the two metaphors. The collaborative and cooperative aspects of LOVE IS A COLLABORATIVE WORK OF ART metaphor are inconsistent (and therefore hide) the aggressive and dominance-oriented aspects of our love experiences as they might be described by "She is my latest conquest," "He surrendered to her," "She overwhelmed me," etc.

By this means, the LOVE IS A COLLABORATIVE WORK OF ART metaphor puts aside some of our love experiences and picks out others to focus on as if they were our only experiences of love. In doing so, it induces a set of similarities between the love experiences it highlights and the real or imagined experiences of collaborating on a work of art.[24]

Metaphors frame the similarities between one set of experiences and another. In doing this, they give shape and meaning to our experiences precisely because they limit our field of vision, orienting us to see some rather than other aspects of our experience, and to do so in one way rather than another.

Metaphors also shape how we act. As Lakoff and Johnson observe, it is one thing to conceive of an argument as a war, another to conceive of it as a dance. Each metaphor shapes how we come to approach the experience of arguing, whether we are to do so aggressively or playfully.

Finally, in structuring our behavior, some metaphors enable us to act more effectively, while others may paralyze us and render us dysfunctional. Thus, not all metaphors are of equal value.

So it is with metaphors for AIDS. They both reveal and hide certain aspects of our experience. They shape the way in which we approach the experience of AIDS. Some metaphors empower people to approach AIDS with a certain gracefulness and determination to live fully and actively; other metaphors (such as Jerry Falwell's "divine punishment" metaphor[25] and Patrick Buchanan's secular counterpart to it: "nature's retribution"[26]) can cripple people with inappropriate anxiety, guilt, and alienation. Not all metaphors for AIDS are of equal value.

Yet, while I am willing to insist along with Sontag that some metaphors (e.g., Falwell's and Buchanan's) must be discarded altogether, the task is, in general, to create and use metaphors carefully and critically, rather than not at all. This requires, of course, that we always have a hermeneutic of suspicion at hand, ready to name the oppressive elements of any given metaphor, the biases and prejudices, and the economic and political interests that have given rise to it. (Sontag's work is of tremendous value in helping us ferret out these destructive elements of certain metaphors.) The task is to construct and find metaphors that are true to the scientific facts about AIDS as best we know them, and that likewise enable individuals and society to cope with this ravaging disease in a graceful fashion by locating it within a meaningful universe. We need to take *both* biological data *and* cultural metaphors seriously. There is plenty of room not only for science, but also for religion and art in this multidimensional task. I am arguing, therefore, for a careful and critical usage of metaphors rather than a rejection of them in toto.

Judith Williamson, film professor at London's Middlesex Polytechnic, writes about an AIDS conference she attended at which one speaker asserted that it was a waste of time "looking at advertising and imagery," i.e., the various ways AIDS is represented in the popular media. What we should confront, the speaker insisted, was *the reality*. Williamson reflects: "But the problem is precisely that our experience of reality is always mediated through structures of meaning which, though by no means immutable, actually have a bearing on what we think *is* real, and how we explain and understand it. These in turn have an effect on what we *do* about it."[27] She is right, of course.

Similarly, it will not do to cavalierly dismiss the religious constructions of AIDS as irrelevant pieties to be tolerated while medical and political professionals go about the "real" work of addressing the epidemic. These religious constructions require our careful scrutiny for, like their biomedical counterparts, they shape us—for better or for worse—and guide our understanding of AIDS and our response to those most affected by it.

As AIDS continues to take its toll on lovers and friends, we will continue to experience fear and outrage, compassion and hope. We will continue to ask "Why?" Something more than a pure biomedical model is needed to sustain us. We need metaphors—carefully crafted and critically employed—to help us make sense out of what is happening to us and those we love.

2 The Catholic Church and the Emergence of Gay Culture

Each incidence of AIDS is a confrontation with every aspect of homophobia—coming out to medical providers, accepting the diagnosis of a fatal illness that is labeled "gay," educating homophobic or just ignorant hospital staffs, fighting for social services and money, convincing biological families that lovers and friends have a right to be at the bedside, working with lawyers on wills and being at funeral homes and memorial services. At each step, there is no escaping the fact that you are gay, that hardly anyone cares about the life or death of a gay person, that the entire system is set up to provide for the needs of heterosexual families, not gay friends and lovers.[1]

AIDS is more than "just a disease." When the Centers for Disease Control first labeled AIDS as "gay-related immune deficiency" (GRID), AIDS became the heir to a vast panoply of metaphors for homosexuality—many of them religiously grounded—that have accumulated in the Western world.[2] "Like a blotter," Kevin Gordon writes, "AIDS has absorbed old, attached, pre-constructed, long-buried associations between sex and sin, sin and death."[3] Homosexuality, already labeled in the West as deviant, was once again seen as leading to death, just as in certain biblical eras sodomy had been seen as a violation of an immutable moral law and therefore punishable by death. So it was that in 1987 Jerry Falwell would write:

God says . . . that homosexuality is a perverted and reprobate lifestyle. God also says those engaged in such homosexual acts will receive "in their own persons, due penalty of their error." God destroyed Sodom and Gomorrah primarily because of the sin of homosexuality. Today, He is again bringing judgment against this wicked practice through AIDS. . . . [H]omosexuals are gaining control of towns and communities. . . . [W]e must preserve America by convicting her of sin and the folly of endorsing a lifestyle that is strangling the very life out of her.[4]

Similarly, the Roman Catholic Cardinal of Philadelphia, John Krol, asserted: "The spread of AIDS is an act of vengeance against the sin of homosexuality."[5] In a more secularized genre, the White House speech writer for Ronald Reagan, Patrick Buchanan, wrote: "The poor homosexuals—they have declared war upon nature, and now nature is exacting an awful retribution."[6] Moralistic metaphors for homosexuality and for homosexual men and women have continued to shape the American understanding of AIDS and our response to it, even despite the fact that, as early as 1982, researchers had discovered AIDS not only among homosexuals and IV drug users, but among Haitians and hemophiliacs as well.

If sociologists Peter Berger and Thomas Luckmann are correct, and our understanding of the world around us is socially generated, then we need to critically examine the processes through which our understandings of AIDS have been generated. And since our metaphors for AIDS have been constructed, to a large extent, out of our inherited cultural metaphors for homosexuality, we turn now to a critical examination of the historical processes that have yielded our current religious, scientific, and popular metaphors for homosexuality in order to shed some light on the ways in which they have influenced our understandings of AIDS.[7]

From Behavior to Condition

Catholic norms regarding homosexuality have their roots in both the Scriptures and Greco-Roman Stoicism. There are, in fact, a variety of sexual metaphors in the Scriptures, such as that found in the older, Yahwist creation account that sees marriage and sexual union as primarily unitive (Eve is created because it is not good for Adam to be alone[8]), and in the Song of Songs, which extols sexual pleasure and physical beauty and love. Nevertheless, the Priestly creation account, in which sex is for the sake of procreation ("be fruitful and multiply"), has been the most prominent in the tradition. The metaphor derived from this latter account presents human sexuality as a matter of complementarity between sexual partners for the sake of reproduction, and thus as inherently heterosexual.

In the Stoic metaphor, sex was likewise directed not to love but to procreation, and therefore an appropriate virtue and decorum were to be observed.

> For the Stoics, intercourse was supposed to take place only so as to produce children. The couple must not make love for the sake of pleasure

alone; even the positions that they adopted should only be those that enabled the seed to be "sown" to best effect. All other forms of lovemaking were a *tolmema*: they were "gratuitous acts." The philosophers regarded them as chilling assertions of an arbitrary freedom on the part of human beings to do what they pleased with their own bodies. The adoption of a variety of sexual positions was a form of playing around in the face of mankind's great Mother, "Nature": "men invented other positions as a result of wantonness, licentiousness and intoxication."[9]

Within this Stoic perspective, you must cultivate *apatheia*, must never fall in love or form a real attachment to anyone. Marcus Aurelius, for example, held that to fall in love is to jeopardize your rational equilibrium, to open yourself up to every misery and to lose all tranquility of soul. Stoic love, therefore, prescinds from all desire for bodily pleasure or immortality and focuses on the requirements of virtue.

Both of these traditions—the biblical and the Greco-Roman—converged in the thinking of the church fathers, especially Augustine, and through them became fully anchored in Western culture. Sex for the sake of pleasure or of love is excluded from this construction of sexuality. Later, St. Thomas Aquinas, drawing from Aristotle, would thus assert that procreation is the natural *telos* of sex, and that homosexual behavior is a lustful indulgence in venereal pleasure since it does not issue in human procreation.[10] It did not occur to Aquinas that there might be a connection between sexual pleasure and love, that one might engage in sex for the sake of love. True love must be sexless, Aquinas reasoned; and it should be focused on the virtue the beloved exemplifies: "The happy man will need these virtuous friends inasmuch as he seeks to study the virtuous actions of the good man who is his friend."[11] The early and medieval Christian and Catholic metaphor for sexuality resulting from this blending of Stoic and Scriptural metaphors thus revealed only a rather narrow range of sexual dimensions, namely, those linked to reproduction. It would be much later before the unitive dimensions of human sexuality would enter the consciousness of prominent theologians.

With regard to homosexuality in particular,[12] John McNeill notes that Aquinas' understanding of homosexuality is a matter of lustful *acts* freely chosen by otherwise heterosexual persons. Aquinas does not understand it as either a biological or psychological condition, a continuous identity of an individual or group, in the way that a twentieth-century Westerner might. This volitional and act-centered understanding of homosexuality became translated into pastoral practice through the use of the penitential manuals in the formation of priests. The pastoral strategy was simply to exhort the penitent to refrain from such acts against nature through the use of his or her free will.

Our contemporary conceptualization of the ethics of homosexuality as a condition did not arise until the end of the nineteenth century when medicine had taken on the role of a forensic science and post-Kantian philosophy had come to stress the subjectivity and freedom of the human person.[13] Yet, sadly, when these new formulations of human sexuality, and homosexuality in particular, were being articulated, the church remained largely immune to them. Indeed, even as late as 1955, Derrick Sherwin Bailey notes in his book *Homosexuality and the Western Christian Tradition*: "I have not carried this general account beyond the end of the Middle Ages because it does not appear that the tradition has undergone any significant alteration since that time—although various legal and other modifications have occurred which have affected judicial practice and, to a limited extent, public opinion."[14] Thus, while other cultural spheres were, over the course of a few centuries, changing and developing their constructions of sexuality in general (and homosexuality in particular) the church did not interact with these changing currents and therefore remained unaffected by them.

This self-imposed isolation from the other cultural spheres has had an obvious influence on the church's response to the AIDS epidemic. As we will see, even during the current AIDS crisis, the American Catholic church, in opposition to the major voices in the psychiatric, medical, and political spheres, has opposed all forms of "safer sex" that could allow for sexual behavior among gay men as well as the use of prophylactics by heterosexual couples. This policy of the church with regard to the AIDS epidemic has been a predictable outgrowth of its traditional sexual metaphor.

Unlike the sexual metaphors of other cultural spheres (e.g., science and law) the Catholic sexual metaphor, as we will see, has undergone very little revision over the centuries. We turn now to examine the modifications that were arising in these extra-ecclesial spheres in order to highlight the gap that would later become so apparent during the AIDS crisis between the Catholic sexual metaphor (and the Catholic metaphor for AIDS) and those of the surrounding culture.

From Sinful to Criminal Act

While there is no evidence that the church itself ever put anyone to death for sodomy or any other reason, nevertheless the medieval power structure did enlist the state as the henchman of the church. "Increasingly," Peter Conrad and Joseph Schneiders point out, "so-called unnatural sexual sins became transgressions against the state. This criminalization of homosexual conduct in the West may be seen as the continuation of a precedent established centuries earlier among the Eastern faithful in Rome and Constantinople."[15]

By the end of the sixteenth century, a power shift had occurred, with the church bureaucracy yielding jurisdiction to the bureaucracy of the state. This did not mean that the religious and cultural articulations of sexual morality were suspended. Rather, the shift simply meant that the state now wielded the power of enforcement of those norms. (Witness, for example, Elizabeth I's attempt to supersede the Church of England and appease Puritan critics in 1558 by establishing the Court of the High Commission to punish sexual offenses that threatened orderly married life. Puritan reformers subsequently effected a more extreme legislation, the Act of May 1, which restored sodomy as an offense punishable by death.) With this shift of jurisdiction from church to state, what had been articulated by the church as a sin gradually came to be understood and treated primarily as a crime.

From Criminal Act to Medically Abnormal Behavior

With the Enlightenment's increased emphasis on rationality, and on science in particular, another important shift occurred. Laws that had previously been established on religious grounds now required rational and scientific justifications in order to maintain legitimacy. From this period on, a *scientific* articulation of sexual normality began to emerge, as physicians were summoned into court to give testimony concerning the culpability of defendants accused of sexual crimes. This forensic employment of scientific medicine gave rise to contemporary sexual discourse and sexology, the scientific scrutiny of sexual behavior. Scientific sexology assumed the role of defining precisely which forms of sexual behavior could be classified as "natural" and "normal."

British sociologist Jeffrey Weeks suggests two decisive influences in the development of this contemporary scientific sexual discourse. The first of these is social Darwinism. Among middle- and upper-class Americans in the latter nineteenth century, physicians influenced by social Darwinism conceptualized the "problem" of same-sex conduct variously as the product of a hereditary predisposition, a holdover from a lower stage of evolution, a "taint" or "degeneration" in the central nervous system. Homosexuality was a condition, a continuous identity found in certain individuals. Departing from earlier moral argumentation, K. M. Benkert, the Hungarian physician who was the originator of the term "homosexuality" in 1869, understood homosexuality as a genetically based condition—a pathological one, indeed, but by no means one involving free choice.

> In addition to the normal sexual urge in man and woman, Nature in her sovereign mood had endowed at birth certain male and female individuals with the homosexual urge, thus placing them in a sexual bondage which renders them physically and psychically incapable—even with the best intention—of normal erection. This urge creates in advance a direct horror of the opposite sex and the victim of this passion finds it impossible to suppress the feeling which individuals of his own sex exercise upon him.[16]

At work in social Darwinism is an essentialist human nature theory that establishes heterosexuality as genetically based. In *The Descent of Man, and Selection in Relation to Sex*, Darwin made the claim that survival of the species depends on sexual selection. The ultimate test of biological success lay in reproduction. "Biology," Weeks writes, "became the avenue into the mysteries of Nature, and its findings were legitimized by the evidence of natural history. What existed 'in Nature' provided evidence for what was human."[17]

As medieval natural law philosophers had reduced sexuality to strictly biological and reproductive metaphors, so now Darwin and his followers made the same case, this time in terms of scientific theories of evolution. The social Darwinists thus assumed a biological literalism not unlike that found in earlier natural law philosophers: sex for the purposes of reproduction. In the context of these Darwinist reproduction metaphors, homosexuality was a degeneration; it did not fall within the range of sexuality as required for the survival of the species. Yet social Darwinism departed from the natural law theorists by asserting that the homosexual aberration was biologically based; it did not result from the free will of the actors as earlier natural law philosophers had argued.[18] Biological rather than moral deficiencies explained the failure to behave heterosexually. Efforts to decriminalize homosexual behavior began to emerge.

The second decisive moment Weeks describes in the emergence of sexual discourse is the appearance of Krafft-Ebing's *Psychopathia Sexualis*: "[I]t was the eruption into print of the speaking pervert, the individual marked, or marred, by his (or her) sexual impulses. The case studies were a model of what was to follow, the analyses were the rehearsal for a century of theorizing."[19] Krafft-Ebing's work greatly influenced Freud, and the former's success gave impetus to the more than one thousand publications that emerged between 1898 and 1908. Out of his "medico-forensic study" of the "abnormal" emerged the taxonomy of sexual pathologies of the late nineteenth century. "Urolagnia and coprolagnia, fetishism and kleptomania, exhibitionism and sado-masochism, frottage and chronic satyriasis and nymphomania, and many, many more, made their clinical appearance via or in the wake of his pioneering cataloguing."[20]

Underlying Krafft-Ebing's foundational work is the Victorian moral code that defined heterosexual procreative sex as normative. Homosexuality, he argued, subverted the "hidden laws of nature" by undermining and confusing the supposedly natural roles of men and women.

Congenital absence of feelings toward the opposite sex.... This defect occurs in a physically completely differentiated sexual type and normal development of the sex organs. There is absence of the psychical qualities corresponding to the anatomical sexual type, but rather the feelings, thoughts, and actions of a perverted sexual instinct. Abnormally early appearance of sexual desire. Painful consciousness of the perverted sexual desire. Sexual desire toward the same sex.... There are symptoms of morbid excitability of the sexual desires, together with an irritable weakness of the nervous system.... The perverse sexual impulse is abnormally intense and rules all thought and sensation. The love of such individuals is excessive, even to adoration, and is often followed by sorrow, melancholy, and jealousy. People afflicted with this abnormality frequently possess an instinctive power to recognize one another.[21]

Indeed, Weeks argues that Krafft-Ebing's painstaking delineation of the "abnormal" was a way of more clearly defining what he and his contemporaries considered "normal." "Krafft-Ebing's 'natural instinct' that 'with all conquering force and might demands fulfillment' is an image of male sexuality whose natural object was the opposite sex."[22]

Thus it was that Michel Foucault could later summarize the nineteenth century shift in the construction of homosexuality as a movement from a type of behavior to a type of personage:

The nineteenth century homosexual became a personage, a past, a case history, and a childhood, in addition to being a type of life, a life form, and a morphology, with an indiscreet anatomy and possibly a mysterious physiology. Nothing that went into his total composition was unaffected by his sexuality. It was everywhere present in him: at the root of all his actions because it was their insidious and indefinitely active principle; written immodestly on his face and body because it was a secret that always gave itself away. It was consubstantial with him, less a habitual sin than as a singular nature.... Homosexuality appeared as one of the forms of sexuality when it was transposed from the practice of sodomy onto a kind of interior androgyny, a hermaphrodism of the soul. The sodomite had been a temporary aberration; the homosexual was now a species.[23]

With the rise of social Darwinism and the work of Krafft-Ebing, the medicalization of homosexuality (and of life itself) was on the march. While this shift toward scientific medicine meant greater freedom from moral and legal stigma for homosexuals (many of the early sexologists such as Krafft-Ebing himself argued for the decriminalization of homosexuality), it was not a purely emancipatory development.

For one thing, the early sexologists betrayed the rather naive faith in science that characterized their age; indeed, they adopted the scientific method as a means of legitimating their work. One of the early pioneers of sexology, Magnus Hirschfield, founded in 1898 the Scientific Humanitarian Committee and later became the founder of the Institute for Sexual Science in Berlin. His watchword was *"Per scientiam ad justitiam,"* and he unabashedly proclaimed: "I believe in Science, and I am convinced that Science, and above all the natural Sciences, must bring mankind, not only truth, but with truth, Justice, Liberty and Peace."[24] Though sexologists have frequently disagreed with each other, they generally have done so on scientific grounds, challenging their colleagues' work as being inadequate from a scientific point of view.[25]

The point to be made here is that our contemporary constructions of sexuality in general, and homosexuality in particular, have been made, at least on the surface, in biological terms and metaphors. Thus, the sexual metaphor employed by medical science highlights the biological dynamics of reproduction, while neglecting other aspects of human sexual experience such as love, commitment, playfulness, and self-transcendence. Biological literalism prevails once again, this time under the legitimating cloak of modern science.

Many of us in this technological era do not share the same undiluted faith in science that Magnus Hirschfield and the early sexology pioneers once had. While science can reliably measure the biological dimensions of sexual experience, it cannot fully account for other elements of that same experience. Such elements require other, nonscientific metaphors derived from art and poetry and religion. We find a need, therefore, to deconstruct the inflated claims of these early scientific pioneers, while relying on metaphors from other spheres of human experience that can account for and make sense out of the broader dimensions of sexuality.

Second, there is clearly a moral quality within this supposedly "objective" and "value-free" scientific project. The first physicians who so described homosexuality as pathological did not seem to be aware that they themselves were heirs of their own culture, whose norms and values they had internalized. Their value-laden conceptualization of homosexuality was derived from their Western, Judeo-Christian tradition. This led to an ironic collusion between modern science and the religious tradition, with the two mutually influencing each other, as is evident in a 1909 article in the French *Revue de l'hypnotisme*, which commented:

> [T]oday we see a curious phenomenon: the Catholic church and Protestant church rank themselves, in relation to homosexuality, on the side of medicine; they declare that sexual inversion is an anomaly of nature, a sickness, and that the paragraphs of the criminal code against the inverts are unjustified.[26]

This link between science and morality would become even more apparent with time, as sexology came to join forces with various social purity movements in Europe and the United States. As late as the 1930s, sexologist Havelock Ellis would write: "At the present time it is among the upholders of personal and public morality that the workers in sexual psychology and the advocates of sexual hygiene find the warmest support."[27] Since sexology was, from the beginning, morally suspect, it behooved the early sexologists to legitimate themselves by aligning themselves with the prevailing moral norms. This has remained the case up to the present time:

> By the 1920s the traditional social purity organizations, deeply rooted as they were in evangelical Christian traditions, were prepared to embrace a cocktail of insights from Ellis and Freud. Today the moral right finds it opportune to legitimise its purity crusades by reference to (selected) sexological findings. Sexology has never been straightforwardly outside or against relations of power; it has frequently been implicated in them.[28]

Value-free science simply does not exist. Buried beneath the early sexologists' claims of scientific "objectivity" lie the inherited moral evaluations and metaphors of the body and sexuality, homosexuality in particular.

During the period we have just reviewed, Catholic moral theology was becoming increasingly isolated and moribund. Following the suppression of the Jesuits, the French Revolution, and the rise of Rationalism, most moral reasoning came to take place within the narrow confines of manuals used in educating the clergy. Very little creative interaction took place between Catholic theology and the larger cultural currents of philosophy and scientific thought.

This isolation of Catholic culture from cultural currents in the larger world went hand in hand with a shoring up of the monarchical and autocratic authority structure within Catholicism. Pope Gregory XVI (1831–46) said: "No one can deny that the church is an unequal society in which God destined some to be governors and others to be servants. The latter are the laity; the former, the clergy." Later, Pius X was even more direct: "Only the college of pastors have the right and authority to lead and govern. The masses have no right or authority except that of being governed, like an obedient flock that follows its Shepherd."[29] Such an authority structure left little room for the presentation and consideration of moral views other than those enunciated by the hierarchy.

It was not until after World War I that creative moral reflection began to relate sexual intercourse to love. The married layman Dietrich von Hildebrand, for example, was the first Catholic theologian to teach that love was a requirement for lawful intercourse. Hildebrand helped set the stage for Pius XI's encyclical *Casti Connubii*,[30] in which the pope wrote that marriage had a twofold purpose, "which is the begetting and education of children for God, and the binding of man and wife to God through Christian love and mutual support."[31] These words represent an expansion of the Catholic sexual metaphor. No longer is sexuality to be understood by Catholic thinkers as purely procreative, but also as unitive, no longer strictly biological, but also personal.

Thus, the Catholic construction of sexuality has become more dynamic, reflecting a tension between these two poles, with writers and officials emphasizing now one pole, now another. This tension in the Catholic construction of sexuality came to shape much of the discussion that would later evolve about homosexuality in particular, with those who oppose legitimating homosexual relations emphasizing the biological pole, and those arguing in its favor emphasizing the personalist pole.

Freud's Ambivalence

With Freud, another dramatic shift occurred within the larger culture's construction of homosexuality. Freud located the foundation of sexuality and sexual orientation not so much in the body as in the psyche of the person; not so much in behavior as in the unconscious thoughts and desires. Neither biology nor society constitutes the human person, but rather a psychic realm in which the biological possibilities of the body acquire meaning. Freud thus broke with the biological literalism of his predecessors. Sexuality for Freud was "a force that is actually constructed in the process of entry into the domain of culture, language and meaning."[32] Left to itself, the human biological makeup carries not a heterosexual determinism, but rather a "polymorphous perversity," a predisposition for bisexuality.

Freud's insistence on the polymorphous predisposition of human beings toward a diversity of sexualities confused the previously clear distinction between homosexual and heterosexual, between masculine and feminine. Both the subjects and the objects of sexual desire were themselves blurred. It was difficult to say which was normal and which perverse. Both heterosexuality and homosexuality are compromises from the polymorphous range of sexual possibilities. "From the point of view of psycho-analysis," Freud wrote, "the exclusive sexual interest felt by men for women is also a problem that needs elucidating and is not a self-evident fact based upon an attraction that is ultimately of a chemical nature."[33]

Freud therefore rejected earlier characterizations of homosexuality as a disease or a congenital degeneration, and he argued for its decriminalization. Moreover, his establishing homosexuality first and foremost as a psychiatric condition brought it even more fully under the jurisdiction of psychiatric and medical professionals. "The therapeutic had triumphed over the religious and legal as the official language to define and explain homosexual conduct and, more to the point, those who engaged in it."[34]

Drawing from the work of such predecessors as Havelock Ellis and Magnus Hirschfield, Freud posited homosexuality as a variation, not a deviation; something different, though not morally bad. It is to be found in persons who "otherwise show no marked deviation from the normal."[35] In a famous letter to a mother who had written to him about her son, Freud summarized his position on homosexuality:

I gather from your letter that your son is a homosexual. I am more impressed by the fact that you do not mention this term yourself in your information about him. May I question why you avoid it? Homosexuality is assuredly no advantage but it is nothing to be ashamed of, no vice, no degradation, it cannot be classified as an illness; we consider it to be a variation of the sexual function produced by a certain arrested sexual development. Many highly respected individuals of ancient and modern times have been homosexuals, several of the greatest men among them. . . . It is a great injustice to persecute homosexuality as a crime and cruelty too.[36]

Freud thus loosened up the traditional heterosexual norm to allow for a fuller "polymorphous" range of normal human sexual experience. Yet in a curious way heterosexuality remains normative for Freud. The polymorphous capacity is shaped in developmental stages as a child interacts with his or her parents and other significant persons. If all goes well in this developmental process, Freud argues, a child will become heterosexual. Adult sexuality thus results from the complex tension between physiological sexual desires, the "libido," on the one hand, and sociocultural prescriptions and proscriptions on the other. Homosexuality represents an arrested stage of development, a failure to successfully navigate the Oedipal complex in which children must manage socially prohibited and threatening incestuous desires for opposite-sex parents. The sexually mature adult successfully weathers these traumas and emerges as a heterosexual. Homosexuality represents an infantile and inappropriate solution to such crises.

Thus, there is a moral ambivalence in Freud's work. On the one hand, he insists on the polymorphous nature of sexuality and a universal predisposition to bisexuality. In this aspect of his theory, he shows an openness to sexual diversity, refusing to label homosexuality as deviant. On the other hand, the developmental character of Freud's theory implies a norm, for his description of the successful human developmental process ends in heterosexual reproductivity. Homosexuality represents an arrested stage of this sexual development. This characterization of human development suggests that certain moral norms are at work in his writing. As Weeks observes, "The difficulty with Freud (especially for someone who wants to believe his critical insights) was that in the end he did believe that a heterosexual genital organisation of sexuality was a cultural necessity, so that although he could readily concede that all of us have 'seeds' of perversion, a healthy development demanded their subordination to the norm."[37] Freud's theory of sexual development was not morally neutral. "Freud slips from analysis to prescription, and the well-organised tyranny of genital organisation becomes the tyranny of psychoanalytic definition."[38] Perhaps this ambivalence explains the subsequent split between his successors, some of whom would see homosexuality as a normal variant, while others would see it as pathological.

Freud's Successors: The Conservative Wing

Those holding the latter, more conservative view saw homosexuality as the cause of great anguish and unhappiness, a pathology for which cures must be sought and attempted. Not only are homosexuals incapable of normal procreation, these thinkers reasoned, but they are also incapable of establishing fully satisfying same-sex relationships. These thinkers developed their conclusions as to the pathological nature of homosexuality not from sociological studies of the larger homosexual population, but primarily from clinical samples of homosexuals who reported enough discomfort to motivate them to present themselves for treatment. Moreover, their pathology definition of homosexuality became extended further into American culture through the military's use of psychiatrists to screen prospective candidates. Those diagnosed by military psychiatrists as homosexual were classified as "psychopathic" and were discharged dishonorably.

Among those most representative of the conservative psychoanalytic tradition are Irving Bieber[39] and Charles Socarides, both of whom have rejected Freud's central notion of bisexuality as having "outlived its scientific usefulness."[40] They both hold for the normativity of heterosexuality. For Bieber, this heterosexuality is biologically based, a "biological norm,"[41] and he thus returns to the biological literalism that characterized the earlier natural law philosophers and pre-Freudian sexologists. Socarides sees sexuality as "anatomically outlined," yet places more weight on the role of cultural evolution: "Heterosexual object choice is outlined from birth by anatomy and then reinforced by cultural and environmental indoctrination."[42] Socarides saw this cultural evolution of that norm as required for survival of the species, and he insisted that to depart from that norm is to court disaster.

Both Bieber and Socarides begin with the assumption that homosexuality is pathological without giving an explanation as to why they hold this view: "all psychoanalytic theories *assume* that homosexuality is psychopathologic."[43] They also have rejected the earlier understanding held by scientists that homosexuality is a condition outside the range of free choice.

> One of the major resistances continues to be the patient's misconception that his disorder may be in some strange way of hereditary or biological origin or, in modern parlance, a matter of sexual "preference" or "orientation," that is, a normal form of sexuality. These views must be dealt with from the beginning.[44]

Both give attention to curing homosexuality, although the results appear rather modest.[45] Bieber claimed that "a heterosexual shift is a possibility for all homosexuals who are strongly motivated to change."[46] His "reconstructive treatment" emphasized exposing the "irrational fears of heterosexuality" and seeking a resolution of those fears.[47] Both he and Socarides regard solid homosexual relationships as out of the question, and homosexual couples as inevitably pained and disappointed. Both derive their samples from clinical populations, that is, from homosexuals who have reported enough discomfort to motivate them to seek treat-

The Catholic Church and the Emergence of Gay Culture **31**

ment. They do not attend to those homosexuals who may report no discomfort or feel no need for treatment. Both Bieber and Socarides focus on the etiology of homosexuality.

Bieber traces homosexuality to the parent-child relationships and early life situations: "An intimate mother-son dyad characterized by restrictive and binding maternal behavior," and, at the same time, a disturbed paternal relationship in which the father is "detached, hostile, minimizing and openly rejecting."[48] Socarides traces homosexuality back even further in the individual's development, to a pre-oedipal phase before the age of three in which the person was unable to separate from the mother and therefore came to assume an inappropriate feminine identity. Socarides' position is thus more extreme than that of Bieber and others since it characterizes homosexuality as "more profoundly pathological than it was generally considered to be when oedipal conflicts were stressed."[49]

Though other psychoanalysts developed differing formulations of the etiology of homosexuality and appropriate treatments to effect its cure, they all agreed with Bieber and Socarides on one thing: homosexuality as a pathological condition. Thus, when the American Psychiatric Association issued its first official listing of mental disorders, *The Diagnostic and Statistical Manual, Mental Disorders* (*DSM-I*), in 1952, it included homosexuality among the sociopathic personality disturbances—that is, those diseases that were considered profound pathologies even though the individuals who have them may experience or report no distress. The *DSM* as revised in 1968 changed the listing of homosexuality from sociopathic personality disturbance to "non-psychotic mental disorder," including it with other sexual deviations such as fetishism, pedophilia, and transvestitism.

It is not difficult to see a similarity between the position of the conservative psychoanalysts and proponents of traditional moral and religious constructions of homosexuality. Both groups work from a human nature theory in which heterosexuality is the unquestioned norm. Both see homosexual behavior as a matter of free choice of individuals and therefore available for either conversion or cure. Finally, both constructions of homosexuality overlook the history of homosexuals as a social group living in a hostile environment and the effects of that environment on their behavior and their psychological and spiritual well-being.

Such a similarity suggests that, as among earlier sexologists, religion and psychoanalysis have continued to influence each other. Even the "value-free" work of scientists and psychoanalysts bears a religious and moral imprint. "Doctors have increasingly turned to technical language and jargon to disguise and suppress their own emotions and underlying values," gay historian Jonathan Katz asserts. "Although secularization has transformed the rhetoric, mystification remains."[50] Moreover, as we will see more fully later, theologians have sometimes engaged in circular reasoning, using this conservative psychiatric construction of homosexuality to justify a conservative theological and moral construction of it as well, all the time overlooking the fact that this psychiatric construction is itself a product of an earlier theological and moral position.

Ironically, partly with the help of the medical community's delineation of homosexual characteristics, large numbers of men and women were able to identify themselves as homosexual. That this identity carried a moral and social stigma did not alter the fact that a definable identity had now become possible. For any given homosexual man or woman, the net effect was a seminal consciousness of being no longer simply an isolated individual with a unique problem, but part of a group with whom one shared a particular sexual identity. The medicalization of homosexuality that began in the late nineteenth century thus had an unintended consequence.

> Ironically, the medical model promoted the articulation of a gay identity and made it easier for many lesbians and homosexuals to come out. In elaborating upon their theories, doctors helped create the phenomenon that most of them wished to eliminate. They transformed an evil impulse that the morally upright strove to resist into the primary constituent of one's nature, inescapable because it permeated one's being. . . . Medical theories made homosexuality not a deed that one avoided but a condition that described who one was.[51]

Freud's Successors: The Progressive Wing

The conservative position as exemplified in Bieber and Socarides has not been the only Freudian construction of homosexuality. The other side of Freud's ambivalence, that which views homosexuality as a normal variant, is represented in the work of such writers as Alfred Kinsey, Cleland Ford and Frank Beach, Evelyn Hooker, and Judd Marmor.

There are a couple of notable similarities in the various works of these latter thinkers. First of all, while remaining well within the parameters of the psychiatric tradition, they remained flexible and open to new data. They were willing to loosen their grasp on previous doctrines in order to allow new questions to be asked, new voices to be heard, and new truths to be discovered. They thereby broadened the definition of what had been considered sexually "normal" by their earlier colleagues. As they attended to the lived sexual and cultural experiences of the population groups they studied, they departed from the inherited biological literalism of earlier scientific and philosophical traditions. The "normal," they concluded, is more varied than an earlier human nature theory had posited. Rather than a deviation from the norm, homosexuality is itself a fully normal variant of human sexuality, every bit as normal as heterosexuality, albeit less frequent among the population. They did not simply assume homosexuality to be pathological as did Bieber and Socarides. Through this flexibility, they became catalysts for growth to occur in their psychiatric community's understanding of homosexuality.

Another similarity among the progressive psychiatrists is the degree to which they were willing and able to engage in quality interaction with the larger homosexual population. To the degree that Kinsey, Ford and Beach, Evelyn Hooker, and Judd Marmor broke out of the usual psychiatric and clinical milieu in order to effectively dialogue with and study homosexual men and women, they began to fashion alternatives to psychiatry's traditional definition of homosexuality as a pathology. Their interaction gave rise to new and broader metaphors for homosexuality.

These writers shifted their attention to the sociocultural constraints that labeled homosexuality as deviant, rather than to the supposedly pathological nature of homosexuality and its etiology. All of these writers were passionately committed not simply to the decriminalization of homosexuality as their scientific forerunners had been, but also to the social acceptance and moral legitimation of homosexual expression.

With the work of these thinkers, it is clear that a definite shift occurred in the psychiatric construction of homosexuality. No longer was there one univocal construction of homosexuality within the psychiatric community. It was no longer possible to say from this point on, as had Bieber in 1962, that "all psychoanalytic theories *assume* that homosexuality is psychopathologic." Serious scholarly (including theological) research into the topic of homosexuality would now have to take this plurality of views into consideration.

Yet a couple of difficulties with the more progressive psychiatric position are worth mentioning. First of all, as Thomas Szaz would later observe, these thinkers have fully accepted the underlying assumption of psychiatric discourse, namely, that biological disease is an adequate metaphor for understanding and treating behavior that runs counter to socially accepted norms, behavior that psychiatrists thus come to label "mental illness." This assumption has allowed psychiatrists to assume virtually the same role previously held by religious and moral leaders, yet to do so under the camouflage of "value-free science," which had become more acceptable in post-Enlightenment Western society. It was the assumption of a moral role by scientists, whether conservative or liberal, that Szaz challenged. Rather than hide behind a supposedly "objective" scientific facade, psychiatrists would do better, Szaz argued, to declare the moral values operative in their diagnoses, thereby making those values available for social scrutiny and discussion.

[I]f moral values are to be discussed and promoted, they ought to be considered for what they are—moral values and not health values. Why? Because moral values are and must be the legitimate concern of everyone and fall under the special competence of no particular group; whereas health values (and especially their technical implications) are and must be the concern mainly of experts on health, especially physicians.[52]

A second problem, this one noted by historian John D'Emilio, stems from the fact that this shifting of the psychiatric metaphors for homosexuality took place primarily on the psychiatrists' own turf, was couched in their own professional terminology, and reflected the interests unique to them and their profession. Homosexuals had not yet found their own voice with which to both articulate and evaluate their experience. Their primary goal was to obtain a degree of social acceptance and respect, particularly in the eyes of the newly established priests of post-Enlightenment culture, the psychiatrists. The interaction between the gay and the psychiatric communities was therefore lopsided, with homosexuals assuming a more or less deferential posture toward the psychiatrists. Had the interaction occurred with greater parity between the two parties, a somewhat different, perhaps less medicalized, construction of homosexuality might have developed. However, as homosexuals came to assume a more politicized sexual identity in the emergence of the movement for gay liberation, they did create new metaphors to describe their experiences and identities.

Homosexuality as a Political Identity

At the same time that a psychological redefinition of homosexuality was taking shape, a new political definition was also emerging for homosexual men and women. With the emergence of industrial capitalism in the late nineteenth century, large numbers of men and women had been pulled out of their homes and farms and into the marketplace. Huge impersonal cities sprang up in which an autonomous personal life became possible. One could now make choices about one's sexual and intimate life, unfettered by traditional family moral codes or economic requirements. This demographic shift made it possible for homosexual men and women both to find each other and to form a group identity. An identifiable homosexual group life became visible in such cities as New York, Washington, D.C., and San Francisco, and included such diverse institutions as bars, cruising areas, and literary societies. Much later, with the outbreak of World War II, this demographic shift intensified even more as large numbers of men and women were brought together in same-sex situations in order to perform military service. This concentration of homosexual men and women continued after the war as discharged military personnel decided not to return home but settled in major urban areas across the country, forming their own literature and institutions. As sociologist John Coleman observes, what anthropologists would call a culture was in the making.[53] With this development, a centuries-long antagonism by the larger culture emerged once again.

The McCarthy-era persecution of homosexuals began on February 28, 1950, when Under Secretary John Peurifoy testified before the Senate Appropriations Committee that most of ninety-one employees dismissed for moral turpitude were homosexuals. Republicans, eager to discredit the Truman administration, sought to exploit Peurifoy's remarks to their own political advantage. In June 1950, the full Senate launched an investigation into the alleged employment of homosexuals "and other moral perverts" in government. The resulting report concluded that homosexual employees of the government were a source of pollution for their coworkers and a threat to national security, almost as great as that posed by communists. The report called for increased enforcement of security measures blocking homosexuals from government employment. In April 1953, President Eisenhower issued Executive Order 10450, which revised Truman's loyalty-security program to include "sexual perversion" as sufficient grounds for exclusion from federal jobs.

In its first sixteen months of operation, the Eisenhower program removed homosexuals from government at a rate of forty per month. By all accounts, however, these figures understate the number of gay men and women penalized for their sexuality. At the very least, they exclude employees still allowed to resign quietly through the compassion of a friendly supervisor. Many more individuals never made it on to the federal payroll, since all applicants for government employment faced security investigations. From 1947 through mid-1950, 1,700 job seekers were denied employment because of homosexuality. After that period, the government expanded its screening procedures.[54]

The military also intensified its efforts to remove homosexual men and women from its ranks. State and municipal governments and private industries under contract with the federal government likewise carried out the effort.

Throughout the investigation and subsequent purge, political officials relied heavily on the pathological definitions of homosexuality as formulated by the conservative wing of American psychiatry. In addition, and rather ironically, "the senators culled information from the Kinsey study of the American male—that homosexual behavior was widespread, that homosexuals came from all walks of life, and that they did not conform in appearance or mannerism to the popular stereotype—in order to argue that the problem was far more extensive and difficult to attack than they had previously thought."[55]

Such was the context in which the Mattachine Society was formed in Los Angeles in 1951 by several male homosexuals who were either members of the Communist party or traveled in left-wing circles. By 1953, Mattachine founders estimated the society's membership to be approximately 2,000. Later, in 1955, a lesbian counterpart emerged with the formation of the Daughters of Bilitis, which, though independent from Mattachine in order to address the issues unique to lesbians, nevertheless worked closely with Mattachine on common issues, sometimes challenging the male membership of Mattachine to be more mindful of lesbians and their concerns.

The founders of Mattachine, particularly Harry Hay, articulated a uniquely gay identity with its own minority group status, its own positive values, and its own reasons for pride in its contributions to the human community. "Victimized by a 'language and culture that does not admit the existence of the Homosexual Minority,' homosexuals remained 'largely unaware' that they in fact constituted 'a social minority imprisoned within a dominant culture.'"[56] In April 1951, the society published a one-page document declaring its purpose to be the unification of isolated homosexuals, their education to see themselves as an oppressed minority, and leadership in the struggle for emancipation. Among the professional backers of Mattachine was UCLA's Dr. Evelyn Hooker, who was just beginning to study male homosexuality with the society's help.

Such a clearly articulated vision proved difficult for Mattachine to sustain in the McCarthy era, especially as its own membership increased to include a diversity of political viewpoints. Thus, in May 1953, a new Mattachine leadership was installed, one that rejected the notion of a homosexual minority and uniquely homosexual culture, and that urged homosexuals to adjust to a "pattern of behavior that is acceptable to society in general and compatible with the recognized institutions . . . of home, church, and state."[57] Moreover, the new officers rejected any collective, militant action by the society in favor of a secondary role in "aiding established and recognized scientists, clinics, research organizations and institutions . . . studying sex variation problems."[58] This often meant relying on the conservative elements of the religious and psychiatric communities with their negative constructions of homosexuality. Thus, for example, Mattachine officers in New York invited a respected psychoanalyst to address them in one of their monthly meetings and he asserted that homosexuality was "an emotional disturbance, . . . a character defense."[59] "In sum," D'Emilio concludes, "accommodation to social norms replaced the affirmation of a distinctive gay identity, collective efforts gave way to individual action, and confidence in the ability of gay men and lesbians to interpret their own experience yielded to the wisdom of experts."[60]

Nevertheless, the 1950s did witness a furthering of homophile identity, and gay men and lesbians did come closer to finding their own voice. Cindy Patton describes some of the features of this earlier gay male and lesbian culture as it was poised on the brink of the revolutionary 1960s:

[W]ith the codification of a sexual culture and fewer demands in terms of the children and spouses of the traditional family constellation, some gay men were at last free to opt for leisure over labor, a choice which allowed for greater participation in sexual activities, social and political organizations—activities which fused the emerging sense of sexual identity with a group identity that would in the late 1960s liken itself to a class or ethnic group. . . . Volunteer time, enthusiasm for community-building, and the good feelings of stabilizing one's community through self-created institutions sent gay men, and to some extent lesbians (who have much different economic restraints), into the creation of churches, physical and mental health clinics, recreation and entertainment, and political organizations.[61]

This newly emerging gay community was also clearly visible in the gay press of the period, in periodicals with such titles as *ONE*, the *Mattachine Review*, and the *Ladder*. Thus, the interactions occurring among gay men and lesbians were slowly intensifying what Clifford Geertz would call a culture: both a worldview (depicting the way gay men and lesbians see things, "their concept of nature, of self, of society") as well as an ethos ("the tone, character, and quality of their life, its moral and aesthetic style and mood . . . the underlying attitude toward themselves and their world that life reflects").[62]

In summary, the 1950s saw a reticent and halting development of gay identity, even despite the constraints imposed by a hostile social and political climate. The homophile movement was also constrained by the fear and internalized homophobia of much of the homophile leadership of the period and a desire to gain respectability within a larger culture that defined homosexuality as beyond respectability. In the interaction between homosexual culture and the structures of politics, as in their interactions with American psychiatry, gay men and lesbians remained deferential, seeking integration and acceptance rather than confrontation. The 1960s would see a dramatic change in the larger social and political climate, and this would have an enormous impact on the ways in which homosexual men and women came to define themselves within the larger American culture.

That larger American culture was undergoing a significant moral shift during the 1950s, but especially into the 1960s, and one element of this shift was the changed valuation given to the erotic. As a result of the psychiatric community's sexual discourse from the eighteenth century onward, the erotic had begun to assume a more central place in the larger culture and in the psychological identity structure of individual Americans, both men and women, heterosexual and homosexual. The liberal sexual consensus that had predominated in the 1950s (which, though not limiting sex to marriage nevertheless saw it as moving toward it, and which had labeled as deviant both homosexuals as well as young mothers who failed to marry) began to unravel.

> By the late 1960s the belief in sex as the source of personal meaning had permeated American society. Aided by the values of a consumer culture and encouraged by the growing visibility of sex in the public realm, many Americans came to accept sexual pleasure as a legitimate, necessary component of their lives, unbound by older ideals of marriage and permanence.[63]

Sex thus became no longer simply something you did in bed, but rather a form of self-affirmation that defined an entire mode of living. Within this larger cultural shift the movement for gay liberation would be both a beneficiary and a key player.

Another element in this American cultural shift was a new spirit of militancy and activism on the part of many Americans. The period saw the formation of the African American civil rights movement in the

South, the anti-war movement, and the women's movement. Throughout the country, people placed a new focus on self-activity as ordinary
women and men sought to speak on their own behalf rather than relying
on the impersonal structures and experts of the "establishment." This
new militancy would affect the gay movement as well. Homosexuals,
rather than deferring to experts and seeking assimilation into the cultural
mainstream, came to assert their rights precisely as homosexuals. Dr.
Franklin Kameny became a leading spokesperson of this new militancy,
and his words marked a decisive break from the accommodationist
homophile leaders of the 1950s:

> I do not see any great interest on the part of the B'nai B'rith Anti-
> Defamation League in the possibility of solving problems of antisemitism
> by converting Jews to Christians. . . . We are interested in obtaining
> rights for our respective minorities AS Negroes, AS Jews, and AS HO-
> MOSEXUALS. Why we are Negroes, Jews, or Homosexuals is totally
> irrelevant, and whether we can be changed to Whites, Christians, or
> heterosexuals is equally irrelevant.[64]

Particularly odious to Kameny and other new gay leaders was the traditional medical model of homosexuality. As Kameny stated in 1964 to
the New York Mattachine Society, "The entire homophile movement is
going to stand or fall upon the question of whether homosexuality is a
sickness, and upon our taking a firm stand on it."[65] An expansion of sexual metaphors and a redefinition of the sexual norm was required,
Kameny argued, if gay men and lesbians were to take their rightful
place in society. In March of 1965, and as a result of Kameny's initiative, the Washington Mattachine Society adopted a resolution stating
"that in the absence of valid evidence to the contrary, homosexuality is
not a sickness, disturbance, or other pathology in any sense, but is
merely a preference, orientation, or propensity, on par with, and not different in kind from, heterosexuality."[66] A new definition of the human
sexual norm was being advanced, one that was less univocally heterosexual, but more open to a variety of forms and expressions. Homosexuality, while understood to be a condition and a continuous identity, was
given a positive evaluation.

Thus, an irony becomes apparent at this point in the story: homosexuals, having become extricated from the oppression of religious moralism with the help of supposedly value-free medical and psychiatric
sciences, now found themselves loosening their ties to those sciences in
order to make an explicitly moral case for the legitimacy of their own
sexual orientation and lifestyle.[67] Crucial to the future of the gay move-

ment was the success with which gay men and lesbians would be able to assert this positive moral evaluation and this expanded, more flexible definition of sexual normalcy, particularly in the medical and psychiatric arenas. Indeed, as we will see in a moment, the conversation continued to be vigorous right up through the dramatic interaction that would occur between gay activists and the American Psychiatric Association in the early 1970s.

Just as some elements of the psychiatric community were showing both a greater willingness to interact with the gay and lesbian community and to loosen some of their own traditional proscriptions, many prestigious attorneys and jurists likewise refashioned their traditional positions. The elite American Law Institute (ALI) completed work in 1962 on a model penal code that eliminated the sodomy statutes. Two years later, the International Congress on Penal Law endorsed the ALI position. Often under the leadership of the ACLU, there was a broadening of support for law reform and civil rights and in the proliferation of court challenges of legalized inequality. In Britain, the 1957 Wolfenden report called for similar reform, and promoted discussion on legal reform throughout the ensuing years on both sides of the Atlantic.

Some elements of the religious community were demonstrating a similar willingness to interact with the emerging homophile movement, and this facilitated a partial reconstruction of the religious metaphors for homosexuality in the United States. Although none of the mainline religious bodies changed their fundamental traditional teaching against homosexuality, a few American church leaders like Episcopal Bishop James Pike called for a separation of morality from law and the elimination of legal prohibitions against private sexual relations. In October 1968, Rev. Troy Perry officiated at the first service of the Metropolitan Community Church, an explicitly gay-positive Christian denomination.

In May 1964, the Glide Urban Center in San Francisco sponsored a four-day consultation between gay activists and Protestant ministers from several cities. The event included a "gay line" tour of San Francisco, including stops at various bars, private parties, drag shows and homophile meetings, and a face-to-face meeting with a group of gay men and lesbians. For many of the ministers, it was the first time they had ever knowingly talked with a homosexual or lesbian. The result was a new sense of cooperation between the two groups and the formation of San Francisco's Council on Religion and the Homosexual (CRH). This cooperation was both tested and solidified when, after police disrupted a CRH-sponsored New Year's Eve dance for the gay community, the ministers held a press conference denouncing the police brutality, a charge that was later sustained in court.

The worldwide Catholic church, at the time, was beginning to demonstrate a similar willingness to interact with the larger culture. Though the Second Vatican Council reaffirmed many elements of traditional Catholic human nature theory, including teachings on sexuality,[68] it nevertheless committed the church to a greater openness to the contemporary world, a willingness to interact with those outside the church, including those in the social sciences. As one decree of the Council stated: "In pastoral care sufficient use should be made, not only of theological principles, but also of the findings of secular sciences, especially psychology and sociology: in this way the faithful will be brought to a purer and more mature living of the faith."[69] A modest hope was thus held out that even the supposedly monolithic Catholic church could change as a result of genuine dialogue with contemporary culture. The prospect held promise for many, both within and outside the Catholic church, including gay and lesbian Catholics and those in the larger gay movement.

Throughout the 1960s, the gay movement continued to interact intensely with the legal, religious, and medical communities. John D'Emilio summarizes developments of that period:

> In the latter half of the 1960s, evidence of change in the law, the clergy, and the mental health profession appeared with accelerating frequency. Activists gained the backing of civil libertarians. They succeeded in opening debate within the churches, continued their attack upon the mental health profession, and saw the authority of the medical establishment rejected by a national task force on homosexuality. Each of these developments made the movement newsworthy, and by the end of the decade, press coverage of gay political initiatives was reshaping public discourse on homosexuality.[70]

The most dramatic event of all, however, took place on Friday, June 27, 1969, shortly before midnight, when two detectives from Manhattan's Sixth Precinct set off with a few other officers to raid the Stonewall Inn, a gay bar on Christopher Street in the heart of Greenwich Village. The officers arrested the bartender, the bouncer, and three drag queens, but when they attempted to arrest one particular lesbian, she put up a struggle. The July 3, 1969, issue of *The Village Voice* reported as follows:

> The scene became explosive. Limp wrists were forgotten. Beer cans and bottles were heaved at the windows and a rain of coins descended on the

cops. . . . Almost by signal the crowd erupted into cobblestone and bottle heaving. . . . From nowhere came an uprooted parking meter—used as a battering ram on the Stonewall door. I heard several cries of "let's get some gas," but the blaze of flame which soon appeared in the window of the Stonewall was still a shock.[71]

While gay history and culture precede the Stonewall riot, nevertheless Stonewall represents the most tangible beginnings of what anthropologists describe as gay culture, with its own set of symbols and meanings, its own ethos and code of conduct. With the Stonewall riot, moreover, the movement for gay liberation took on much larger and more visible proportions. From this point on, the construction of a metaphor for sexuality in general and for homosexuality in particular was no longer strictly the project of religious, civil, or psychiatric professionals. Gay men and lesbians had now become active participants in shaping those metaphors. From now on, the experiences and reflections of gay men and lesbians would have to be considered a necessary and integral part of any construction of homosexuality and any credible sexual discourse.

Notable throughout this period was the continued interaction between the increasingly activist gay community and the mental health community. Irving Bieber, Charles Socarides, and other proponents of the sickness model of homosexuality reached the high point of their influence during the late 1960s, and made their presence felt in court cases and other legal battles. Yet the first stirrings of change were beginning to appear. In September 1967, the National Institute of Mental Health appointed Evelyn Hooker to chair a committee charged with investigating the subject of homosexuality. The committee's final report clearly parted ways with the traditional pathological view and asserted a more expansive sexual metaphor, noting that human sexuality extended across a continuum of behavior. It argued that tolerance of those persons who were already gay was the best social policy.

The post-Stonewall vigor of gay culture and "Gay Power" soon became evident in interactions with the American Psychiatric Association over the classification of homosexuality on the APA's list of mental disorders. On December 15, 1973, the APA's board of trustees decided to delete homosexuality from the second edition of its *Diagnostic and Statistical Manual of Psychiatric Disorders* (*DSM-II*).

What became clear throughout the APA's arduous deliberations was the political and cultural nature of psychiatry's construction of homosexuality. Once again it became clear that psychiatric constructions of illness are not purely a matter of objective, value-free, scientific truth. They are also a matter of inherited cultural norms and values and a product of the interaction of political interests vying with each other for hegemony.

> Because concepts of mental health and illness are so intimately linked to prevailing sociocultural standards of appropriate behavior, it is not surprising that in a period characterized by challenges to those standards, psychiatry would be beset by internal confusion and controversy. But it is precisely at such moments that the profession acquires a degree of relative autonomy. Freed from the strictures of hegemonic and unquestioned standards, it may side either with the still-dominant norms of behavior or with the values that inspire critical and challenging social forces. That freedom, relative independence, and power become, however, sources of grave difficulty. With the normative foundations of its work made manifest, the posture of value-neutrality becomes untenable. Psychiatry is forced to assume a partisan role.[72]

The APA's 1973 decision marked a decisive shift within the American mental health profession. The American Psychological Association soon followed suit. The American mental health community in general has continued to maintain a favorable construction of homosexuality.

In various ways, similar interactions continued to take place with the other cultural spheres as well, particularly regarding the question of gay civil rights. The struggle against criminalization of homosexual behavior won the support of the American Bar Association and the American Medical Association. Religious groups as diverse as the Society of Friends, the Lutheran Church in America, and the National Council of Churches joined in these efforts as well.

The Formulation of the Official Catholic Position on Homosexuality

Within Catholic circles during this period, a number of significant developments occurred: Dignity, an organization of gay and lesbian Catholics was formed, and many Catholic leaders spoke out in behalf of gay civil rights, including the National Federation of Priests Councils, the National Coalition of American Nuns, and a number of prelates including Philadelphia's John Cardinal Krol and Detroit's John Cardinal Dearden. Moreover, a national social survey of the period from 1972 to 1985 showed increasing support among American Catholics for gay civil rights, though not for gay sexual activity. George Gallup, Jr., and Jim Castelli, reflecting on their research during that period, wrote:

In general, Catholic acceptance of homosexuality in society has increased in the past decade. There are a number of explanations for the high degree of tolerance among Catholics. One stems from the fact that Catholics are a minority themselves, and while they are certainly less aware of minority status than they once were, they are aware enough to be sensitive toward other minorities.[73]

On the level of official moral teaching and directives for pastoral care, however, the Catholic church during this period reaffirmed its traditional proscription of homosexual sexual expression. Moreover, overtures made by the Second Vatican Council to dialogue with contemporary culture provoked a reaction within the magisterium itself, the official teaching body of the church.

Thus, ten years after the Council, in the same period that had seen the deliberations of the American Psychiatric Association regarding homosexuality, the Vatican's Sacred Congregation for the Doctrine of the Faith noted that "erroneous opinions and resulting deviations are continuing to spread everywhere," making it necessary to publish an authoritative though not infallible "Declaration on Certain Questions Concerning Sexual Ethics." This document, the first to deal with the pastoral and moral issues of homosexuality, represents a strong reaffirmation of Catholic human nature theory. Rather than seeing human nature and moral norms as socially constructed and therefore somewhat fluid, the "Declaration" speaks of "an objective moral order," and "the immutable principles based upon every human person's constitutive elements and essential relations—elements and relations which transcend historical contingency."[74] The document includes traditional Catholic sexual ethics as part of the church's immutable teaching.

> Since sexual ethics concern certain fundamental values of human and Christian life, this general teaching equally applies to sexual ethics. In this domain there exist principles and norms which the church has already unhesitatingly transmitted as part of her teachings, however much the opinions and morals of the world may have been opposed to them. These principles and norms in no way owe their origin to a certain type of culture, but rather to knowledge of the divine law and of human nature. They therefore cannot be considered as having become out of date or doubtful under the pretext that a new cultural situation has arisen.[75]

The "Declaration" accepts the psychiatric conclusion that homosexuality for many people is a condition that is constitutive of a given person and for which there is no cure. In doing this, it draws a distinction between a moral evaluation of this condition and that of homosexual acts. It encourages pastoral sensitivity for those with a homosexual condition, insisting that the culpability of such people "will be judged with leniency." At the same time, it condemns the acts themselves as "intrinsically disordered." The task for the homosexual man or woman is to exercise his or her free will in order to make the best of a bad situation.

Drawing on the conclusions of the conservative wing of American psychiatry (and overlooking the fact that those conclusions are themselves products of an earlier religio-moral code) the "Declaration" describes the homosexual condition as pathological. It rejects the more progressive conclusions later adopted by the APA, and speaks disparagingly of those "who, basing themselves on observations in the psychological order, have begun to judge indulgently, or even to excuse completely, homosexual relations between certain people."

Overall, the "Declaration" reaffirms the dual sexual metaphor found in Pius XI's *Casti Connubii*, insisting that moral standards for human sexuality must "preserve the full sense of mutual self-giving and human procreation in the context of true love."[76] It reasserts that "according to the objective moral order, homosexual relations are acts which lack an essential and indispensable finality," and are, according to the judgment of Scripture, "intrinsically disordered." Given its understanding of the homosexual condition and homosexual behavior as disordered, the "Declaration" concludes that pastors should not counsel homosexuals to form relationships analogous to marriage.

The Consolidation of an American Gay Culture

On the other side of the Atlantic, however, the gay movement and culture continued to unfold. Gay men and lesbians, with a new sense of self-confidence, began constructing their own identity and making their own rules regarding sexual practice. This identity and lifestyle was constructed in a variety of ways, from the "fast-lane sex" of the bath houses and sex clubs (the "sexual laboratories," as Foucault called them)[77] to demands for recognition of "gay marriages." Moreover, this identity expanded to include far more than the strictly sexual, as evidenced in a proliferation of gay professional, social, and political organizations, a growing body of gay literature at both the scholarly and popular level, and a growing appreciation of a buried culture that included Proust and Tchaikovsky, John Maynard Keynes, and Leonardo da Vinci and Michelangelo.

This culture has continued to develop through its interactions (and frequent clashes) with other groups on the American political horizon. Battles have been fought against the efforts of Anita Bryant in Dade County, Florida, John Briggs in California, and the New Right as it emerged during the Reagan years under the leadership of such men as Jerry Falwell. Gay San Francisco supervisor Harvey Milk was assassinated. Civil protection on the basis of sexual orientation has come to be included in hate-crime ordinances of city and state governments, and, in some cities (e.g., Seattle, Berkeley, and San Francisco) and some corporations (e.g., Lotus, Levi-Strauss), gay and lesbian couples can officially register their relationships as "domestic partnerships," affording them the same financial benefits given to heterosexual married couples. Gay and lesbian leaders are currently on record as opposed to the Boy Scouts' policy of excluding gay members. The multicultural aspect of the gay community is becoming more articulated thanks to the development of gay/lesbian organizations of Asians, African Americans, Native Americans, and those of other racial and ethnic heritages. In the first year of Bill Clinton's presidency, the question of whether openly gay men and lesbians could serve in the military dominated the headlines, as did new genetic theories about the origins of homosexuality. Later, the historic convergences of several hundred thousand gay rights marchers in Washington, D.C., in 1993 and in New York in 1994 showed the power and diversity of a community coming of age.

Such historical experiences have shaped and refined gay culture. What had begun as a "lifestyle enclave" composed of gay men seeking sexual pleasures within their private lives has now become what Robert Bellah and colleagues would call an emerging community.[78] Today, this gay community as found, for example, in San Francisco, has an entire institutional complex including four political clubs, its own health services, and two rival weekly newspapers. For many years now, moreover, San Francisco has been notable for gay political involvement in neighborhood, environmental, educational, labor, arts, and civil-rights issues—issues extending beyond the advancement of purely gay self-interests. One thinks of gay county supervisors Harvey Milk and Harry Britt, and Roberta Achtenberg and Carole Migden, who have been leaders in a wide range of progressive causes including height limitations on buildings, rent control, and animal control, among other issues. Finally, the gay community has become increasingly a "community of memory," as gay scholars have begun retrieving a heretofore lost history in much the same way that scholars within African American, Japanese American, and other minority communities have done.[79] Anthropologist

E. Michael Gorman, moreover, is able to list several other symbolic elements and rituals that have emerged within this gay universe:

> Some historical symbols of gay culture are the pink triangle, the rainbow flag, Harvey Milk, San Francisco and the Stonewall Inn Riots, which story itself attains mythic character. Related to these symbols, both encapsulating and concretizing them as part of the culture, are the rituals and social processes intrinsic to the constellation of the gay world. These rituals and processes include coming out, gay pride parades, political demonstrations, and the establishment of gay identified territorial communities or "ghettos."[80]

Moreover, the more recent AIDS crisis as it unfolded throughout the 1980s and up to the present has likewise shaped this culture. Given the fact that the usual interpreters of disease—scientists, physicians, government officials—were unwilling to invest themselves in the AIDS epidemic, the gay community filled the vacuum, coming to own the disease in such a way as to become "the single most powerful force in the struggle against AIDS."[81] This meant that the other groups within the crisis, when they did enter the struggle, were forced to negotiate with the gay community in order to gain legitimacy and the necessary resources. This role of the gay community as the chief player in the initial American construction of AIDS has also had its effects on the gay men themselves, forcing them to redefine gay identity in less exclusively sexual terms and more around the political, cultural, and health care aspects of the AIDS struggle itself.

Thus, in the 1980s, many gay institutions and rituals became established and solidified around the need to address the epidemic. One thinks of the annual Memorial Candlelight March commemorating those who have died in the epidemic, the NAMES Project Quilt, and the rituals that are included as an element of volunteering at any of a host of AIDS service agencies.

The Vatican's 1986 "Letter to the Bishops of the Catholic Church on the Pastoral Care of Homosexual Persons"

Despite the continued articulation of gay culture and identity that had taken place in the 1970s and 1980s, the Vatican position hardened against it even more. Eleven years after issuing the "Declaration," the Vatican's Congregation for the Doctrine of the Faith feared that "in the discussion which followed the publication of the Declaration . . . an overly benign interpretation was given to the homosexual condition itself, some going so far as to call it neutral, or even good." This fear resulted in the "Letter to the Bishops of the Catholic Church on the Pastoral Care of Homosexual Persons," a document corrective in tone and purpose, written in English, apparently with the American church in mind. Like the "Declaration" before it, this "Letter" describes the particular inclination of the homosexual as not sinful, yet goes a step further, asserting that it is "a more or less strong tendency ordered toward an intrinsic moral evil; and thus the inclination itself must be seen as an objective disorder."

Also like the "Declaration," the "Letter" shows an ambivalence toward the social sciences. Thus, on the one hand, it acknowledges that "the Church is in a position to learn from scientific discovery" and it presents its teaching as in accordance with "the more secure findings of the natural sciences, which have their own legitimate and proper methodology and field of inquiry." On the other hand, the "Letter" does not limit its teachings to the conclusions of the social sciences, for, as it states, the church's moral position is based not on scientific reasoning alone, but rather "on human reason illumined by faith." The church thus "transcend(s) the horizons of science."

This posture on the part of the Congregation has prompted reactions from many Catholic thinkers. Lillian Kopp, for example, sees the "Letter" as exhibiting "academic fraud" and a betrayal of the impulse earlier articulated by the Second Vatican Council to seriously interact with the social sciences.

Such appearance of disdain for interdisciplinary and interdenominational teamwork and of reliance on prescientific data is a scandal in the magisterium, not just because it is the epitome of conservative fundamentalism —a diversity the church can countenance—but also because the letter fails to thereby acknowledge that, over and above Scripture and tradition, the Spirit of Wisdom continues to enlighten and direct humankind through the scientific mode of revelation and the *sensus fidelium*. The letter repudiates, in effect, Vatican II's Pastoral Constitution on the Church in the Modern World where bishops of the church affirmed that "in pastoral care, appropriate use must be made not only of theological principles, but also of the findings of the secular sciences, especially psychology and sociology," in order to "blend modern science and its theories and understanding of the most recent discoveries with Christian morality and doctrine" (*Gaudium et Spes*, no. 62).[82]

The "Letter" shows a similar unwillingness to interact with the gay movement itself, which, by 1986, had become one of the major political and social outcomes of the sexual revolution in the American scene. In 1984, two years prior to the "Letter's" publication, American Catholic sociologist John Coleman had argued that no interpretation of homosexuality could be considered credible if it bypassed the moral and religious claims that had been generated by the gay movement itself. Coleman further asserted:

> Minimally, the task for the churches would seem to be to sift carefully and discern the moral and religious claims implicit in this self-generated hermeneutic of homosexuals. Because of its theological claims to correlate Christian tradition with human experience, it would seem impossible to achieve a genuinely modern Christian hermeneutic for homosexuality if dialogue (which is never the same as mere acceptance) with the moral and religious claims of homosexuals is simply bypassed.[83]

Yet bypassed it was, as these words of the "Letter" indicate:

> Nevertheless, increasing numbers of people today, even within the Church, are bringing enormous pressure to bear on the Church to accept the homosexual condition as though it were not disordered and to condone homosexual activity. Those within the Church who argue in this fashion often have close ties with those with similar views outside it. These latter groups are guided by a vision opposed to the truth about the human person, which is fully disclosed in the mystery of Christ. They reflect, even if not entirely consciously, a materialistic ideology that denies the transcendent nature of the human person as well as the supernatural vocation of every individual.
>
> The Church's ministers must ensure that homosexual persons in their care will not be misled by this point of view, so profoundly opposed to the teaching of the Church.[84]

In keeping with this refusal to interact with homosexual groups or movements, the "Letter" directed that "all support should be withdrawn from any organizations which seek to undermine the teaching of the Church, which are ambiguous about it, or which neglect it entirely."[85]

With regard to the civil order, the "Letter" decries the violence directed at homosexual persons as revealing "a kind of disregard for others which endangers the most fundamental principles of a healthy society." Yet it equally decries any civil legislation that regards homosexuality in positive terms or fails to regard it as disordered. Ironically, the "Letter" ends up virtually condoning the very violence it condemned: "When such a claim is made and when homosexual activity is consequently condoned, or when civil legislation is introduced to protect behaviour to which no one has any conceivable right, neither the church nor society at large should be surprised when other distorted notions and practices gain ground, and irrational and violent reactions increase."[86] Arguing within the framework of traditional Catholic moral theology, John Coleman responds to the inadequacy of the "Letter" regarding gay civil rights:

> Laws which discriminate against homosexual people strike me as perpetrating such great moral evil that they should be resisted on traditional Catholic grounds. In *We Hold These Truths*, John Courtney Murray argued that laws against contraception would involve a greater evil of state intrusiveness into bedrooms. A similar logic would apply to the private acts of consenting homosexual adults. It is clear, to me at least, that a classic and traditional case can be made for Catholic support for civil liberties for homosexual people. In this respect, I find the recent CDF letter quite untraditional.[87]

Thus, the "Letter" reasserts the traditional Catholic sexual metaphor. It discourages any serious interaction with either the social sciences or the gay movement or civil libertarian movements within the civil order. So much for the promise held out by the Second Vatican Council for interaction with the larger world.

Both the "Declaration" and, later, the "Letter to the Bishops" stimulated vigorous discussion among many Catholic thinkers. One of the more visible participants in this discussion was John McNeill, S.J., whose 1976 book *The Church and the Homosexual* called for a broader Catholic sexual metaphor that would include homosexuality as a normal variant. After a protracted struggle with Jesuit and Vatican officials, the book was published in 1976 with an *imprimi potest*. However, two years later, the Vatican Congregation for the Doctrine of the Faith ordered the Jesuit Superior General to withdraw the *imprimi potest* and to prohibit McNeill from lecturing on issues of homosexuality or sexual ethics. Several years after this silencing, McNeill was further ordered by Jesuit superiors, on the insistence of the Vatican's Cardinal Ratzinger, to "withdraw from any and all ministry to homosexual persons," an order McNeill felt he could not in conscience obey.[88] Shortly after McNeill refused to cease his own ministry within the gay/lesbian community, the Vatican issued its "Letter." McNeill publicly protested the "Letter," thereby breaking his public silence, an action that, in turn, finally prompted his Jesuit superiors to dismiss him from the religious order.

The response to the "Letter" by the larger American church, bishops included, has likewise been equivocal. (One conservative bishop I once spoke with referred to the "Letter" as "an embarrassment.") Formal discussions within the National Conference of Catholic Bishops have often attempted to blunt the "Letter's" harsher edges concerning homosexuality.[89] And although the Vatican has condemned any interaction with the gay community, interaction has indeed continued in a variety of quiet, informal ways.

Many priests, despite the prohibitions of some (though not all) local bishops, have continued to minister to such groups as Dignity, the outlawed organization of American gay and lesbian Catholics. Moreover, in some dioceses such as Seattle and San Jose, where the Vatican directive to expel Dignity from church property technically has been implemented, the relationship between the local hierarchy and the local gay community has remained both cordial and mutually supportive. Pastoral action thus continues to be, in many parts of the United States, a locus of interaction between Catholicism and the gay culture.

Yet another skirmish between the Vatican and the gay community emerged on June 25, 1992, as a result of a document entitled "Some Considerations Concerning the Catholic Response to Legislate Proposals on the Non-discrimination of Homosexual Persons" released to the U.S. bishops by the Office of the General Secretary of the Congregation for the Doctrine of the Faith. This document was a reaction to legislation in parts of the United States and Italy that has outlawed discrimination on the basis of sexual orientation or made public housing available to gay couples. The document rejects the idea that sexual orientation is a protected category, like race, sex, age, or religion. It summarized the earlier documents in their assertion that homosexuality is a disordered inclination, and homosexual sexual expression is not a human right. The documents concluded: "There are areas in which it is not unjust discrimination to take sexual orientation into account, for example, in the consignment of children to adoption or foster care, in employment of teachers or coaches, and in military recruitment" (Section II, paragraph 11).

This Vatican document elicited strong protest from members of the church, a reaction that could well bode a shift in relations between the American church and the Vatican as well as in the American Catholic construction of homosexuality. Several bishops, including Archbishop Daniel Pilarczyk of Cincinnati, Archbishop John Quinn of San Francisco, Archbishop Thomas Murphy of Seattle, Bishop Thomas Gumbleton of Detroit, Archbishop Rembert Weakland of Milwaukee, and Cardinal Joseph Bernardin of Chicago, have publicly distanced themselves from the Vatican statement. Three bishops, along with 12,400 other Catholics, signed a protest statement entitled "A Time to Speak: Catholics for Gay and Lesbian Civil Rights," sponsored by New Ways Ministry and several other progressive Catholic organizations. The fact that so many priests, nuns, and laity—and yes, even bishops— responded in such an outspoken manner may indicate an unraveling of Vatican control over American Catholic moral discourse on homosexuality.

One final, though more delicate, issue in the Catholic/gay relationship arises from the fact that many Catholic priests are themselves gay and participate in many of the rituals and practices of gay life.[90] That this has become apparent to many in the gay community in recent years is evidenced in the cover story of the February 4, 1986, issue of the gay newsmagazine *The Advocate*. The front page headline for the article read: "Catholic Hypocrisy: If So Many Priests Are Gay, How Can the Church Be So Homophobic?"

The Catholic Church and Gay Culture: The Importance of Learning to Listen

Cultural metaphors are constructed through the interaction of individuals and groups in society. Because AIDS was first regarded as a gay disease, and because the gay community came to play a preeminent role in the American discourse on AIDS, our metaphors for AIDS and those for homosexuality have mutually shaped each other. Our inadequacies in constructing one of these realities will render inadequate our construction of the other. Likewise, the American Catholic metaphors for AIDS have been shaped by Catholic metaphors for homosexuality. In this chapter we have traced and critically assessed the process through which those latter homosexual metaphors have been constructed.

Throughout most of the period when much of Western culture was reformulating its understanding of human sexuality, the Catholic hierarchy operated within a self-imposed isolation, forbidding the introduction of new ideas into Catholic life from either the social sciences or from the church's laity. More recently, the hierarchy has emphatically refused to interact with progressive social science and with gay culture in formulating a homosexual metaphor. This has meant that the church has either been left out of the picture in the generation of homosexual metaphors by the larger society, or, worse, named as an enemy. At the same time, the church's own homosexual metaphors are less credible because the church has not assimilated through dialogue the wisdom that the social science and gay communities can provide. This has two unfortunate consequences, one for the internal life of the church, and the other with regard to its effectiveness as a moral agent within the larger culture.

With regard to the internal life of the church, it has become a truism to say that American Catholicism's theory of human sexuality is making less and less sense to many contemporary Catholics. As we have seen, especially since the 1950s, many contemporary Americans, including American Catholics, have come to see sexuality as an integral element of a fully human life, and sexual satisfaction as necessary for personal happiness. The demands arising from such a cultural shift have even become unofficially institutionalized within the American Catholic landscape in groups like CORPUS (resigned and married Catholic priests urging a change in the mandatory priestly celibacy policy), Catholics for Free Choice (advocating women's abortion rights), and Dignity. As this cultural change in the level of expectations for sexual fulfillment increasingly comes to define the American temperament, more and more men and women will find themselves outside the moral boundaries established by the present Catholic sexual metaphor. A weakened affiliation with the church becomes more likely. Indeed, Andrew Greeley has insisted that a weakened affiliation—ranging from complete withdrawal to less frequent mass attendance, from decreased financial generosity to an unwillingness to encourage sons and daughters to become priests and religious—has already occurred among American Catholics as a result of church teachings on birth control and the role of women in society.

Thus, this cultural shift poses a challenge for the internal life of American Catholicism, as it would for any set of traditional norms and rules. Edward Shils suggests:

> The ground for survival [of a tradition] is the accumulation of and steady presence of evidence of the efficacy of adherence to the rule of conduct. When the wants of individuals change and more is demanded than was previously regarded as satisfactory, then adherence to the traditional rule might not be able to produce results at the higher level now desired. . . . The rules which permitted actions leading to the previous level of satisfaction will then be discredited.[91]

Unless American Catholicism is able to assimilate such increased levels of desire for sexual fulfillment on the part of its own members, it will be that much less able to maintain their strong affiliation, particularly if they happen to be gay. As one theologian asserts, "The prevalent meta-phors have not been informed by what many gays and lesbians consider to be homosexuality's potential for human dignity and fulfillment. Until the homosexual experience is truthfully spoken and respectfully heard, the church will be unable to stand in the truth, endure it, and live from it."[92]

The current intransigence of the bishops on the issues of safer sex and condoms has further weakened the bishops' credibility. That the American bishops, even in the midst of this deadly epidemic, have, for the sake of the present narrow sexual metaphor, denounced the few (al-though limited) tools at our disposal in combating the spread of the HIV virus suggests that the current Catholic homosexual metaphor has now become dysfunctional rather than life-serving—for Catholics and non-Catholics, gays and heterosexuals alike.

But the church is not the only loser here. Also at stake is the larger American culture that, in the absence of a credible Catholic voice, is less likely to develop an adequate construction of sexuality.

As I mentioned earlier, the construction of sexuality as it has emerged in the larger Western culture over the last two centuries has had its own inadequacies, largely because it has been overly medical-ized. Medical science alone simply cannot account for the full range of dimensions to be found within human sexual experience. That experi-ence is not simply a matter of biology or emotional and physical satis-faction. Often it is also one of self-transcendence involving genuine love and care, self-sacrifice, lasting commitment, and loyalty. Our available stock of sexual metaphors must allow us to acknowledge not only the biological and psychological healthiness of our sexual relation-ships, but also their sacredness—and this is as true for gay men and les-bians as it is for heterosexuals. Other metaphors, including religious ones, are required if we are to make sense out of the various dimensions of sexuality. Traditional Christianity, with such treasures as the Song of Songs and the Yahwist creation account, can thus play an invaluable role in offering sexual metaphors that will both critique and complement the medical and psychological metaphors currently available to us within American culture.

The inability of American Catholicism to bring the richness of its own tradition to that effort means that the larger American culture, par-ticularly the gay and lesbian community, is that much poorer. Thus, for the sake of its internal life as well as for the sake of the larger culture, the American church would do well to attend to its metaphors for homo-sexuality. Catholic theologian Xavier John Seubert says it well:

Suppressing the metaphorical process stifles the life of the organism which more often than not remains out of touch with its greatest potentials. I think that this is the situation in which the Roman church finds itself today. Its tradition offers a rich network of metaphors; but only certain metaphors have been employed by the magisterium with regard to homosexuality, and even these have been interpreted in terms of a physical literalism that limits their content. This, as I see it, is at the heart of the church's difficulties with sexuality in general and homosexuality in particular.[93]

The construction of a more adequate Catholic metaphor for homosexuality, and therefore for AIDS, would require a dual effort. First of all, theologians and church leaders would need to loosen up the currently narrow and ossified Catholic sexual metaphor. This would mean recognizing that much of the Catholic sexual ethic is a social construct, a product of earlier social and cultural interactions. As such, it merits the same careful and mature reflection we give to other such constructs. This loosening process would require a willingness to honestly examine certitudes once thought to be unchangeable, allowing new questions to be asked, new data to be assimilated, new voices to be heard.

We have reviewed the story of how a similar process occurred within the medical and psychiatric construction of homosexuality. Through this process, a fuller and richer psychiatric construction of human sexuality became possible. We also saw how a similar loosening of the Catholic sexual metaphor has occurred before (as evidenced in *Casti Connubii*) in response to the movements within modern philosophy. Such a process seems warranted today, given the cultural shifts within the erotic sphere, but especially in the face of AIDS.

A second element of this constructive effort would be a more conscious interaction with the broader range of social scientific opinion, as well as with the gay community itself. The gay community has played, in the absence of other responsible voices, a very prominent role in the American construction of AIDS. Any credible construction of AIDS by the Catholic hierarchy must therefore be one that emerges out of genuine interaction with the gay community. This interaction would require an attentive listening to recent scientific findings beyond those of psychiatry's conservative wing. It would need to overcome the suspicion of academic fraud that some critics have held.

This interaction also would require attention to the lived experience of gay men and lesbians, *both* as individuals *and* as a culture. Since the gay and lesbian movement has become a bona fide culture and political entity in its own right, church leaders cannot be content simply to interact with individual gay men and lesbians in the confessional or the rectory parlor. As occurred earlier within the mental health community, interaction also needs to take place on a more formal level, with recognized leaders and thinkers from within the gay community (and today, with recognized leaders of the AIDS community as well).

On this cultural/political level, the interaction would need to be a mutual process and involve a mutually critical assessment of each party's symbols and values, a recognition of the legitimate and positive elements of each, and, when appropriate, an assimilation of those positive elements of the other culture into one's own. From a Catholic perspective, theologian Richard McCormick describes some of the dimensions of this listening:

> First, listening as a part of teaching can refer to the inescapable need to consult all sources of knowledge and wisdom before one draws normative conclusions. This would seem to be obvious to anyone who rejects a quasi-magical notion of the church's magisterium. As [Archbishop Rembert] Weakland words it: "The Church's need to listen is no exception."
>
> The second understanding of listening as a part of teaching is that one teaches *by listening*. The very act of listening is itself instructive and enlightening, and indeed about the very matters that constitute the concern of listening. What I have in mind, of course, is that the teacher who sincerely and genuinely listens communicates many things: a sense of the dignity, worth and importance of those listened to; a sense of the honesty, openness and humanity of the teacher; a sense of the realism, importance and limitations of the teaching itself. These "senses" render us much more docile and favorably disposed to what is ultimately concluded. We might say that such "senses" help us to see more clearly.[94]

The construction of a more adequate Catholic homosexual metaphor would require the kind of listening McCormick describes.

Such an interaction does not require the church to abandon its traditions and values, fully discarding its own identity.[95] Somewhere between an absolute refusal to interact with the gay culture and a complete and uncritical assimilation of it there lies, I am willing to wager, the possibility of a mutually enriching conversation. The choice is not between the inherited tradition and the latest politically correct fashions, but rather between a tradition that has become rigid and strangling for many people and one that remains flexible enough to live and grow. Opting for a living tradition would require a willingness to interact in a genuine way with other contemporary cultures, including the gay culture. Only such a living tradition is capable of speaking a life-affirming, challenging, and credible word to contemporary American culture in this tragic time of AIDS.

3 The American Catholic Bishops and the Social Construction of AIDS

Metaphors for AIDS abound. This epidemic has been constructed as a divine retribution, an instance of passive genocide, a modern plague, a millennial disease, the disease of our times, a holocaust. That this should be the case is both inevitable and necessary as we human beings struggle to give shape and meaning to this tragedy.

As any other culture must do when confronting this crisis, American Catholicism likewise generates its own metaphors for AIDS. Uniquely Catholic metaphors therefore emerge, both on an official level of episcopal teaching as well as on "the streets" where pastoral workers struggle to make sense out of this epidemic and to meet the needs of people with AIDS and their caregivers. In the next chapter, I will look at the metaphors that have emerged from the work of some of those pastoral caregivers. In this chapter I want to focus more on the metaphors generated at the official level in the two statements of the American Catholic bishops: "The Many Faces of AIDS: A Gospel Response," issued by the Administrative Board of the United States Catholic Conference on December 11, 1987, and "Called to Compassion and Responsibility: A Response to the HIV/AIDS Crisis," issued by the National Conference of Catholic Bishops on November 9, 1989.

Not all AIDS metaphors are of equal value. Some metaphors reveal and account for more elements of our experience than do others. Some spark our imaginations, revealing for us wonderful possibilities we previously overlooked. Some enable us to experience a richness of emotion that makes us more fully alive and leads us to act more gracefully and effectively in the world. Some metaphors are, in short, more adequate than others. The question of discernment therefore arises: how do we differentiate between adequate and inadequate metaphors? What criteria do we use? It is important for us to reflect critically about such AIDS metaphors—both Catholic ones and those generated from other cultures—to carefully discern those that are adequate from those that are not.

I first want to suggest criteria we can use as rules of thumb for measuring the adequacy of our metaphors for AIDS, including those generated from within American Catholicism. While there are many legitimate angles from which one could develop such criteria, I will argue here in favor of criteria that serve human values, both social and personal. In this view, a metaphor functions like a map: it is adequate if it gets us where we want to go; it is inadequate if it does not. Thus, I believe that the ethicist Albert Jonsen is correct in asserting that those who work with metaphors for AIDS have an important role to play in defeating the epidemic, "because the pictures they paint in their minds and in the minds of the public will direct public attention, mobilize public energy, modify public behavior, and generate public money. The public language . . . of AIDS is as important as the science."[1]

I propose, then, the following three criteria for measuring the adequacy of AIDS metaphors: (1) Does the given metaphor empower us in our efforts to end the epidemic? (2) Does it contribute to social cohesion in the face of this crisis? (3) Does it enable individual persons with AIDS to live with dignity, determination, and grace?

In proposing these three criteria, I am aware that metaphors are necessarily limited creatures, only more or less adequate. Nevertheless, some metaphors will meet these three criteria more fully than others. I am merely suggesting here a framework for discussing and discerning their adequacy. Moreover, I am suggesting that a more adequate AIDS metaphor will satisfy all three of these criteria, though it may meet one criterion more fully than the others.

Let me, then, present each of the three criteria one at a time, describe some of its implications for evaluating our metaphors, and then apply it to the official construction of AIDS offered by the American Catholic bishops.

Does the AIDS Metaphor Empower Us in Our Efforts to End the Epidemic?

AIDS activist Douglas Crimp writes: "We don't need a cultural renaissance; we need cultural practices actively participating in the struggle against AIDS. We don't need to transcend the epidemic; we need to end it."[2] Accordingly, this first criterion reflects a concern for both *biomedical* and *political* efficacy.

On the *biomedical* side, this first criterion requires us to take the biological facts seriously, paying careful attention to the very specific bio-logical processes through which the human immunodeficiency virus is transmitted and the means that can arrest them. Any valid AIDS meta-phor must correspond to the best medical data we have available.

This criterion would therefore rule out, for example, those scientifi-cally untenable metaphors that regard AIDS as an essentially gay dis-ease. (Perhaps this misperception was understandable in the early years of the epidemic when immunology and epidemiology had given the dis-ease the unfortunate label GRID, i.e., gay-related immune deficiency. The medical construction of the disease has moved beyond that earlier misperception, however, especially with the discovery of the virus that underlies the immunological disorder. The medical focus has therefore shifted from a particular population group to specific behaviors capable of transmitting the virus, behaviors not necessarily unique to gay men.)

This criterion likewise rules out AIDS metaphors that reflect a fear of human sexuality. (The issue, as virologists now know, is not sex itself, but what kinds of practices and safeguards one utilizes while having sex.)

Similarly, this criterion excludes an overly facile construction of the disease that would label as sick (and therefore uninsurable and unem-ployable) an asymptomatic and otherwise perfectly healthy person with HIV. Likewise, this criterion excludes metaphors that imply that AIDS is communicable through casual contact. In short, this first criterion re-quires taking seriously the biomedical aspects of AIDS.

This criterion also calls our attention to questions of *political* effi-cacy. Metaphors for AIDS frequently imply various political solutions to the crisis, whether it is quarantining, HIV testing, or campaigns for safer sex. Some metaphors more effectively spark our political imagina-tions and harness our energies than do others. For example, as San Fran-cisco General Hospital's Jan Zita Grover notes, it is one thing to under-stand AIDS in terms of war, and a very different thing to perceive it in terms of preventing contamination. The war metaphor implies a com-mon alliance against an enemy that threatens us all and whom we hope eventually to win to our side. It calls for personal sacrifice and allows for failures along the way toward final victory. It evokes a rich tapestry of images and stories from historical wars: "the Trojan Horse, pyrrhic victory, crossing the Rubicon, the Holocaust, the second (or third) front, colonial wars, tactics, strategies." By contrast, the contamination meta-phor does not look toward an eventual victory over the enemy, but rather, "its goal is to keep the other side as far away from us as possible, to keep it as unlike us as possible."[3] The difference between the two metaphors is both subtle and crucial. One could make the case, in evaluating these two metaphors according to this first criterion, that the "War Against AIDS" metaphor is relatively more adequate than the second; it can more effectively harness our political energies to halt the spread of the epidemic than can the metaphors of contamination.

Now let us apply this criterion to the American Catholic bishops' construction of AIDS. Both of the bishops' statements apply many elements of the traditional Catholic human nature theory to AIDS, and this application results in a uniquely Catholic construction of this epidemic. It is a multifaceted understanding of human nature and of AIDS that is at work here. In accord with traditional Catholic human nature theory, the bishops place a definite value on modern medicine and technology while simultaneously maintaining a critical distance from them. They also place great value on concerns of justice regarding people with AIDS. The general context of their reflections is a larger human nature theory that includes certain convictions concerning human dignity— including human sexuality—as well as more pragmatic concerns to end the epidemic.

Let us examine first of all their approach to the biomedical aspects of AIDS. On the one hand, their confidence in biomedicine is apparent in both documents. Thus, they insist that "AIDS is an illness to which all must respond in a manner consistent with the best medical and scientific information available."[4] They applaud the fact that "the medical community has developed therapies which extend the lives of people with HIV infection while enhancing their quality. New discoveries raise hopes for the eventual cure or prevention of the disease."[5] They also recognize, however, that there is much more to learn both about HIV itself and about "whether current strategies for controlling the spread of the virus are working."[6]

The bishops provide and demonstrate a working knowledge of the basic biological aspects of HIV infection that play themselves out in both individuals and population groups.[7] They are aware that it is more than simply a gay disease, that it "cuts across all racial and ethnic lines," that it especially threatens Hispanic and African American communities, and that it cannot be contracted through ordinary casual contact.[8] They correctly see the disease as a matter not of population groups, but of specific practices: "AIDS, in other words, is a human disease whose spread, according to the best available scientific knowledge, is limited to identifiable modes of communication and contact."[9] Moreover, in their second statement they incorporate the insight of the 1988 report of the presidential commission, which acknowledges that "[t]he term *AIDS* is obsolete. *HIV infection* more correctly defines the problem,"[10] because it calls attention to the full course of the disease rather than simply its final stages.[11]

They acknowledge that education programs must reflect accurate medical information[12] and they lament the fact that "[l]ack of education about HIV in large segments of the society fosters continued misunderstanding about the epidemic. For example, confusion about how the infection is transmitted generates some unwarranted fear and undue alarm."[13] They go even further, however, committing "ourselves and our resources, within our moral restraints and prudent judgment, to provide education to limit the spread of AIDS and to offer support for persons with AIDS." And while they insist that any AIDS education that warrants their support must be situated within an adequate moral context, they nonetheless assert: "Pertinent biological data and basic information about the nature of the disease is essential for understanding the biological and pathological consequences of one's personal choices, both to oneself and others."[14] They insist on the need "to discuss publicly the direct link between sexual activity and intravenous drug use on the one hand and AIDS on the other. Silence about the connection between these forms of behavior and AIDS is not only intellectually dishonest, but it is unfair to those at risk."[15] They welcome the fact that "[t]he surgeon general of the United States has provided careful analysis of the causes of AIDS, the ways in which it is transmitted and the various dangers or risks of contracting the disease."[16] In short, the bishops share in the overall American confidence in scientific medicine.

Yet they are not naive about biomedical technology. Indeed, the bishops' second statement laments: "Technology often outpaces ethical reflection; the study of ethics is widely neglected in school curricula."[17] Clearly, the efficacy of medical technology is not the only value the bishops have in mind when it comes to this epidemic. In both documents, they repeatedly insist that AIDS cannot be adequately understood in biological terms alone: "In our view, any discussion of AIDS must be situated within a broader context that affirms the dignity of the human person, the morality of human actions, and considers the consequences of individual choices for the whole of society."[18]

To state it somewhat differently, the bishops are framing their contribution to the larger American discourse on AIDS in terms of their own cultural values and biases. In constructing the AIDS crisis in this way, the bishops are in harmony with some of the major currents in contemporary social reflection. Many contemporary social critics, such as those in the Frankfurt school, have called our attention to what they perceive as a growing "technocracy," a facade of inexorability surrounding modern technical developments that blindly assumes we are forced to employ them regardless of human choice or their usefulness in enhancing human and global well-being. Such critical theorists have insisted on the need to reassert the primacy of human values and human freedom over modern technology. In an analogous fashion, the bishops unabashedly hope to interject into the larger American AIDS discourse the religious and ethical values embodied within the Catholic human nature theory.

> We, the Catholic bishops of the United States, approach this task from the perspectives of faith and reason: faith, which believes that health and sickness, life and death have new meaning in Jesus Christ; and moral reasoning, which supports the insights concerning human nature and individual dignity which we here affirm. We address this statement to the Catholic community and to all people of good will. It is our hope that these reflections will stimulate discussion and foster understanding of the ethical and spiritual dimensions of the HIV crisis.[19]

Thus, in the eyes of the bishops, technical solutions must be evaluated in light of other human values.

This broader moral context is likewise integral to the way the bishops approach the issue of *political* efficacy in ending the epidemic. They are concerned to address "the moral dimensions of public policy":[20]

> In sum, it is our judgment that the best approach to the prevention of AIDS ought to be based on the communication of a value-centered understanding of the meaning of human personhood. Such a perspective provides a suitable context for the consideration of legislation or educational policy.[21]

This moral concern governs the wide array of political critiques, observations, and proposals they offer, all of which reflect various cultural values within American Catholicism.

With regard to the political dimensions of the epidemic, the bishops regard as normative such things as "reach[ing] out in compassion to those exposed to or experiencing this disease," and "stand[ing] in solidarity with them and their families."[22] It likewise regards as normative efforts to eliminate "the harsh realities of poverty and despair" frequently surrounding this disease.[23] It asserts that human life has an absolute sacredness: "God's gift of life is precious, and there is more to life than its sometimes depressing or superficial elements."[24] It seeks to balance the claims of individual rights with the rights of society as a whole.[25]

More specifically, the bishops' construction of AIDS "call[s] upon
all in the health care and support professions to be mindful of their general moral obligation, while following accepted medical standards and
procedures, to provide care for all persons, including those exposed to
the AIDS virus."[26] It points out the need for adequate housing for
PWAs,[27] "decr[ies] the exclusion of certain groups of persons from
health insurance coverage,"[28] and insists that persons with AIDS continue to be employed as long as it is appropriate.[29] The bishops note that
the AIDS crisis has exemplified "the weakness of our health care deliv-
ery system," and add: "This problem must be addressed in a way that
will provide adequate and accessible health care for all."[30] Their second
statement calls for increased collaboration between government and private agencies in drug testing and education as well as in meeting health
and human service needs for HIV positive people. Moreover, it states
boldly: "Federal funding for AIDS care remains insufficient."[31]

The bishops call for making HIV testing available (though not mandatory), informing people that they are being tested when donating
blood, informing them of test results and providing them with pre- and
post-test counseling.[32] Disclosure of test results to those other than the
person tested can only occur legitimately under strict conditions.[33] In
short, both documents speak amply to the question of political efficacy,
and do so within the moral context of the Catholic social justice tradition.

One significant debate within the American AIDS discourse that the
bishops leave unaddressed has to do with the search for the "magic bullet." Since virologists discovered the virus believed to underlie the disease we now call AIDS, much scientific research has focused on finding
a cure, a "magic bullet," to knock out that virus. This has been pursued
often at the expense of providing services to those already suffering
from the disease and other efforts to develop effective treatments for the
opportunistic diseases (e.g., pneumocystis carinii pneumonia, candidiasis) to which those with suppressed immune systems are susceptible.
One is left wondering, after reading the two documents, whether the
bishops' moral reflections could have shed some light on this important
dilemma.

Included within the broader moral worldview of the bishops are
uniquely Catholic values pertaining to human sexuality, and it is here
that their construction of AIDS becomes particularly interesting and
controversial. As Berger and Luckmann have noted, every culture has
its own sexual program. The culture of the American bishops is no ex-
ception. Their sexual program—in which "heterosexuality is norma-

tive"[34] and "[s]exual intercourse is appropriate and morally good only when, in the context of heterosexual marriage, it is a celebration of faithful love and is open to new life"[35]—clearly governs their construction of AIDS.

As the British anthropologist Mary Douglas might have predicted, and as religious and moral leaders have done in earlier outbreaks of sexually transmitted diseases,[36] the bishops view AIDS as one more perilous effect resulting from deviations from the established Catholic moral norm for sexuality. Douglas describes the pattern here:

> [T]he ideal order of society is guarded by dangers which threaten transgressors. These danger-beliefs are as much threats which one man uses to coerce another as dangers which he himself fears to incur by his own lapses from righteousness. They are a strong language of mutual exhortation. At this level, the laws of nature are dragged in to sanction the moral code: this kind of disease is caused by adultery, that by incest. . . . The whole universe is harnessed to men's attempts to force one another into good citizenship. Thus we find that certain moral values are upheld and certain social rules defined by beliefs in dangerous contagion, as when the glance or touch of an adulterer is held to bring illness to his neighbors and children.[37]

AIDS thus provides the bishops with another opportunity to rearticulate and promote the traditional Catholic sexual program:

> [W]e are convinced that unless, as a society, we live in accord with an authentic human sexuality, on which our Catholic moral teaching is based, we will not address a major source of the spread of AIDS. Any other solution will be merely short term, ultimately ineffective and will contribute to the trivialization of human sexuality that is already so prevalent in our society.[38]

That the bishops see the AIDS epidemic as a moment in which to reaffirm and promote the traditional Catholic sexual ethic is readily apparent. One is struck by the fact that so much of both episcopal statements is taken up with a rearticulation of the common Catholic themes of sexual abstinence, chastity, monogamy, and the ban on contraception. Their use of the epidemic in this way also appears in the failure to make important distinctions between sex that is unsafe and sex in general. An example:

> We fault these ["safer sex"] programs for another reason as well. Recognizing that *casual sex is a threat to health*, they consistently advise the use of condoms in order to reduce the danger. This is poor and inadequate advice, given the failure rate of prophylactics and the high risk that an in-

fected person who relies on them will eventually transmit the infection in this way. [My emphasis][39]

That "casual sex," though a violation of Catholic moral codes, is necessarily "a threat to health" is not, in fact, medically established. What *is* a threat to health from a medical standpoint is *unsafe* sex, casual or otherwise, with a potentially infected partner. We can lament the breakdown of traditional sexual mores; but we have no clear medical evidence that this breakdown necessarily contains medical risks. From a technical and medical standpoint, the bishops fail to grasp adequately the dynamic involved here. The failure makes one suspicious as to their true motive—whether it is simply to prevent the spread of AIDS or to use the epidemic as a weapon to wage a moral crusade against the liberalization of sexual mores within the larger American culture. Indeed, the latter seems all the more plausible given Cardinal Ratzinger's May 29, 1988, letter to papal nuncio Archbishop Laghi in response to the bishops' first statement. In that letter, Ratzinger refers to "the real cause of the problem, namely the permissiveness which, in the area of sex as in that related to other abuses, corrodes the moral fiber of the people."

Unfortunately, this episcopal construction was summarized by two American prelates in the naive and hackneyed slogan "Good morality makes good medicine," an assertion that both Catholic ethicists and AIDS activists alike have justifiably seized upon and challenged. As some of these critics have observed, it is conceivable that a Catholic woman, wishing to follow her bishops' sexual norms to the letter, could find herself having unprotected sex with her HIV-positive husband, thereby putting herself at risk of infection. By contrast, a sexually active gay man may have umpteen sexual partners every night of the week, clearly in violation of the bishops' norms, yet remain safe from infection if he carefully practices safe sex. Good morality, at least as it is defined by the American Catholic bishops, does not always make good medicine. Given that the stakes involved in this kind of unnuanced thinking are human lives, one biomedical ethicist has remarked: "In my view, the church's credibility and intellectual integrity are at risk. Beyond question, so are human lives, perhaps in great numbers."[40]

Now for the controversial issue of condoms. In the development of the bishops' specific teaching, a significant shift occurred. The first statement, issued by the United States Catholic Conference, allowed for a presentation of very circumscribed information about condom usage within public education programs. The second statement made no such allowance. It is worth tracing the difference between the two documents.

When the first document addresses those who are HIV-positive, it reads:

> Earlier we stated something of the meaning and purpose of human sexuality. If a person chooses not to live in accord with this meaning or has misused drugs, he or she still has the serious responsibility not to bring injury to another person. Consequently, anyone who is considered "at risk" of having been exposed to the AIDS virus has a grave moral responsibility to ensure that he or she does not expose anyone else to it . . . and should act in such a way that it will not bring possible harm to another.[41]

Following this admonition, the bishops address the case of the infected person who is not willing to abide by that moral responsibility. They invoke the teaching concerning the counseling of the lesser evil that, traditionally, has been permitted on two conditions: "(a) The person counseled is determined to commit and prepared for the commission of the greater evil; and (b) there is no other way of preventing the greater evil."[42] Thus, their carefully circumscribed allowance of education regarding prophylactics:

> Because we live in a pluralistic society, we acknowledge that some will not agree with our understanding of human sexuality. We recognize that public educational programs addressed to a wide audience will reflect the fact that some people will not act as they can and should; that they will not refrain from the type of sexual or drug abuse behavior which can transmit AIDS. In such situations educational efforts, if grounded in the broader moral vision outlined above, could include accurate information about prophylactic devices or other practices proposed by some medical experts as potential means of preventing AIDS. We are not promoting the use of prophylactics, but merely providing information that is part of the factual picture. Such a factual presentation should indicate that abstinence outside of marriage and fidelity within marriage as well as the avoidance of intravenous drug abuse are the only morally correct and medically sure ways to prevent the spread of AIDS. So-called safe sex practices are at best only partially effective. They do not take into account either the real values that are at stake or the fundamental good of the human person.[43]

Going still further, and speaking to those working in Catholic hospitals, the first statement reads:

It would be permissible . . . to speak about the practices recommended by
public health officials for limiting the spread of AIDS in the context of a
clear advocacy of Catholic moral teaching. On the more personal level of
the health care professional, the first course of action should be to invite a
patient at risk, or one who already has been exposed to the disease, to live
a chaste life. If it is obvious that the person will not act without bringing
harm to others, then the traditional Catholic wisdom with regard to one's
responsibility to avoid inflicting greater harm may be appropriately applied.[44]

As I mentioned in the Introduction, following issuance of that first
statement, and prompted by erroneous media reports that the church was
softening the traditional Catholic ban on contraceptives, many conservative prelates, especially New York's Cardinal O'Connor, loudly objected. The bishops of Metropolitan Washington likewise asserted:

[T]he document has been interpreted to mean that in effect pastors and
health care professionals can counsel those who are infected with AIDS
and who are determined to remain sexually active to use condoms. That
position too must be rejected. It is never morally permissible to employ
an intrinsically evil means to achieve a good purpose. No Catholic pastor
or counselor is ever free to advocate the use of contraceptive devices.[45]

Consequently, the second statement, this time issued by the National
Conference of Catholic Bishops, asserted simply that "advocating this
approach means in effect promoting behavior which is morally un-
acceptable."[46] Thus the second statement gave less leeway to the discussion of condom usage.

The strength of cultural biases becomes readily apparent whenever
we look at those areas where our knowledge is uncertain. This is certainly true when we ask ourselves about the technical effectiveness of
condoms in halting the spread of the epidemic. The technical answer is
not clear, at least on a practical level: Correct use of a condom, while
giving a definite degree of protection, cannot give one hundred percent
assurance that one will not become infected.[47] The answer one gives to
this question of the efficacy of condoms is therefore likely to depend to
at least some degree on one's own cultural bias rather than exclusively
on technical information.

Thus, the condom itself becomes constructed variously by different
people, depending on their values and interests.[48] From the standpoint of
condom manufacturers, a condom is a source of potential financial in-
come. They are likely to defend the prophylactic effectiveness of condoms if doing so will yield them the highest profit. From within the sci-

entific, "value-free" worldview of modern Western medicine, condoms are scientifically proven to have a definite, though limited, effectiveness when used correctly. Thus the surgeon general defines them as "the best preventive measure against AIDS besides not having sex and practicing safe behavior."[49] From the standpoint of many gay men a condom is likely to be a means of continuing to enjoy their sexuality (a right they have long fought for) in these days of the epidemic. They are therefore likely to view them as technically effective in slowing the spread of the virus.

Within the culture of the American bishops, by contrast, the condom is a tool for sexual deviance. It is a form of birth control,[50] and in the case of gay men, a means of facilitating their immoral sexual activity. In a more extreme view, as we have seen in the words of the bishops of Metropolitan Washington, a condom is an "intrinsic moral evil" that can never be used for a legitimate moral purpose.[51] When the bishops condemn the use of condoms in this fashion, they are making a *moral* claim, but one that governs their apprehension of the technical facts regarding the efficacy of condoms.

Thus, not surprisingly, the bishops, having constructed the condom to be immoral, also find it to be technically ineffective: "The use of prophylactics to prevent the spread of HIV is technically unreliable."[52] In fact, promotion of condom usage fosters "a false sense of security and actually lead[s] to a greater spread of the disease."[53] Thus, even though the "best medical and scientific information available" has convinced the surgeon general and other health experts that condoms are effective enough to warrant their promotion and proper use, the bishops, given their cultural biases and values, won't buy it.

The point here is this: the bishops' construction of AIDS, and their corresponding views regarding condoms, can be neither fully understood nor successfully challenged simply in terms of "facts." For underlying their position on AIDS and condoms is the sexual program of their culture, and it is their adherence to this program that shapes how they view such questions as the technical efficacy of prophylactics.[54] It is fundamentally a matter of cultural values here, not scientific and technical "facts."

What needs to be addressed, moreover, is not whether the bishops' own cultural values and biases should govern their discussion of the technical efficacy of condoms. Of course they should. Values and cultural biases, as the Frankfurt school suggests, clearly should govern discussions as to which technologies are to be employed. Moreover, it would be naive to think that cultural values and biases should somehow not shape the perceptions of bishops—as they do those of other human beings—regarding the efficacy of proposed technical solutions. Our wrestling with such questions is always culturally shaped, and never dispassionate and value-free.

Nevertheless, what does need careful scrutiny is the *validity* of the particular cultural norms the bishops are applying to this discussion. More pointedly, in this particular discussion we need to ask, as have so many in recent years, How valid is the Catholic sexual ethic, particularly its ban on artificial contraception and its construction of homosexuality? Until that question is adequately dealt with by the American Catholic bishops, their subsequent position on whether condoms should be promoted in halting the spread of AIDS will inevitably remain problematic and inadequate.

Unfortunately, the general body of American bishops does not appear willing to address the Catholic sexual program at this time. Although a significant number of the bishops privately disagree with the Vatican's traditional ban on artificial birth control (including condoms), the 1990 National Conference of Catholic Bishops' statement on human sexuality reinforced the traditional teaching. The consequences of this teaching with respect to the AIDS epidemic are, unfortunately, measured in the number of human lives lost.

From a biomedical standpoint, and given the scarcity of adequate medical means for halting the spread of AIDS, the bishops' position can only be regarded as irresponsible. Simply to counsel sexual abstinence for gay men, the unmarried, and those with HIV-infected spouses is, quite frankly, not a responsible public health policy within contemporary America. Moreover, from the standpoint of the gay community, the bishops' forbidding of condom usage can only be construed as one more instance of an oppressive rigidity and homophobia.

Does the American Catholic bishops' construction of AIDS empower us in our efforts to halt the spread of this epidemic? From a political standpoint it certainly does. It draws from a rich and passionate social justice tradition that capably addresses a wide range of elements that make up our experience of AIDS. From a more biomedical standpoint, however, the bishops' construction of AIDS is inadequate. While condoms are a reasonably effective tool—one of the few currently available to us—in stemming the spread of the virus, the bishops refuse to condone their use. They do this, we can surmise, primarily for the sake of a sexual ethic that most American Catholics and many of the bishops themselves no longer agree with but are either unwilling or unable to openly discuss.

Perhaps Bishop Kenneth Untener of Saginaw is correct. During that 1990 meeting of the American hierarchy in which they reaffirmed the traditional teaching on birth control, he courageously suggested that the bishops at least discuss that teaching. The logic of that teaching, he asserted,

> is not compelling. It is not compelling to the Catholic laity, not compelling to many priests and not compelling to many bishops. When we know this and don't say it, many would compare us to a dysfunctional family that is unable to talk openly about a problem that everyone knows is there.[55]

Does the Metaphor Contribute to a Dynamic Social Cohesion in the Face of This Crisis?

In June 1987, Ryan White's family finally moved out of Kokomo, Indiana, where they had lived for several difficult years. "I didn't want to die there," Ryan had told his mother. "I really didn't want to be buried there." In the previous few years, Ryan had been vilified on local radio talk shows as a "faggot" and a "queer." His family's car had been pelted with eggs and its tires slashed. Someone had fired a bullet through their living room window. The story of Ryan White's social ostracization is now well known; it is a tragic reminder of the unnecessary pain wrought by fear and discrimination in this epidemic.[56]

This second criterion assumes that it is better for society to hold together in the face of this crisis rather than to become fragmented. It counters the individualism that sociologist Robert Bellah and colleagues are justifiably concerned about, a cultural phenomenon unfortunately in abundance in the early years of the Reagan administration when what we now refer to as AIDS was first identified. Moreover, it implies that a crisis of this magnitude can only be addressed if there is an all-out, focused, and disciplined collective effort, personal self-sacrifice on the part of individual citizens, and heroic leadership on the part of political officials.

David Kirp, in *Learning by Heart*, his book about schoolchildren with AIDS, writes in the concluding chapter:

> If the spread of AIDS is to be slowed, cooperation is necessary between the infected and those still untouched. This means, at least, self-restraint on the part of people who carry the virus and an end to discrimination by those who don't. An every-person-for-himself individualism, a devotion to self-interest narrowly construed, a denial of responsibility to the im-

pact of one's conduct on one's neighbors: that attitude, if it came to domi-
nate, could all too literally spell the death of many of us. The need for
cooperation to ensure survival is why communities of compassion . . . are
not just Sunday school pieties but powerful weapons in the war on AIDS.
It is why communities of isolation . . . will ultimately fail to protect their
members—and, in the process, be corroded by fearfulness and distrust.[57]

Yet social cohesiveness does not mean social uniformity. AIDS, as
I suggested above, cannot be legitimately used to bludgeon diverse
cultures and individuals into a single uniform ethical code. The formation of a coherent national and social purpose vis-à-vis the AIDS epidemic does not have to occur at the expense of a legitimate and valuable
diversity.

If the United States is, as sociologists describe it, a society of
societies—each with its own legitimate and unique identity yet part of a
larger whole—then AIDS metaphors should reflect the pluriform character of our country. Thus, this second criterion emphasizes a necessary
communion and mutual responsibility among citizens, yet one that respects the legitimacy and richness of a diversity of cultures.

Accordingly, this criterion rules out metaphors that construct the epidemic in terms of "we-they," and that portray people with AIDS, particularly gay men and intravenous drug users, as "contaminated others"
who are somehow outside the nation and somehow distinct from a supposedly uniform "general population." It insists that HIV-positive
people, and the diverse communities of which they are members, are
themselves a legitimate part of that general population. It likewise rules
out metaphors that focus on a medically unfounded fear of contamination by these "others" (sometimes referred to as the "high risk
groups," often meaning immigrants, gay men, women, the poor, and racial minorities) and that lead to such discriminatory practices against
them as exclusion from school and workplace.

This second criterion rules out metaphors that disregard the medical
(and moral) imperative for safe and responsible sexual behavior. While
this does not have to imply the "erotophobia" that some AIDS activists
fear,[58] it does acknowledge that the necessity of social cohesiveness in
the face of this epidemic has forced us as a culture to rearticulate the
rules for sexual behavior. The necessary cultural goal here is not to become less sexual but rather sexual in new ways that will not jeopardize
bodily health, mutual trust between partners, and the common good.

Finally, this criterion requires us to pay special attention to the very
process of constructing metaphors and the social contexts out of which
the various AIDS metaphors have emerged. Richard Goldstein, arts edi-

tor for the *Village Voice*, has noted the vast difference between AIDS metaphors constructed by the popular American media and those generated by PWAs and openly gay artists. The former have often emphasized that "both the virus and its carriers must be kept at bay,"[59] whereas the latter have emphasized the bonding among gay men, the comfort afforded the person with AIDS by the gay community, and the need for dissent and struggle to end the epidemic—very different metaphors emerging from very different social sources. Those framed in interaction with persons with AIDS are likely to be very different from those framed in interaction with unaffected Hollywood film producers concerned about ratings.

Thus, we need to critically examine the social and cultural sources of any given AIDS metaphor. We need to ask questions about those who generated it: Who are they? What are the norms and values of their cultural context? What are their political and economic interests? With whom are they interacting as they create and adopt their various metaphors? Likewise, when we ourselves set about the creative task of generating metaphors for AIDS, we need to pay careful attention to our own cultural influences and interests as well as to the people with whom we are interacting since our metaphors will be shaped accordingly.

This second criterion bears directly on the two statements of the bishops. Clearly, a central theme in Catholic social teaching is that of human community. This was so clear, for example, in the U.S. bishops' pastoral on the economy, "Economic Justice for All," in which they stated so simply: "Human life is life in community."[60] It is likewise a predominant theme in the bishops' statements on AIDS. In contrast to alternative constructions of persons with AIDS as "other," the bishops write:

> Persons with AIDS are not distant, unfamiliar people, the objects of our mingled pity and aversion. We must keep them present to our consciousness as individuals and a community, and embrace them with unconditional love.[61]

Indeed, the bishops base their commonality with persons with AIDS on a simple, shared humanity and the fact that all of us are mortal:

> [T]he Gospel acknowledges that disease and suffering are not restricted to one group or social class. Rather, the mystery of the human condition is such that, in one way or another, all will face pain, reversal and ultimately the mystery of death itself.[62]

The bishops' vision of human community is theologically grounded in the ministry of Jesus, who "with compassion . . . breaks through the barriers of sickness and sinfulness in order to encounter and heal the afflicted."[63] They see in the traditional Christian doctrine of the Trinity a model for human community: "that we become most fully ourselves by giving ourselves to others."[64] Theirs is an organic understanding of human community in which all are members of one another, such that "[a]n abuse of self is somehow also an act of injustice to others; and, by the same token, the abuse of others is an abuse of self and an abuse of our relationship with God, the Creator and Father of us all."[65] They quote Pope John Paul II's words during his 1987 visit to San Francisco's Mission Dolores Basilica:

> [T]he love of God is so great that it goes beyond the limits of human language, beyond the grasp of artistic expression, beyond human understanding. And yet it is concretely embodied in God's son, Jesus Christ, and in his body the church . . . God loves you all, without distinction, without limit. He loves those of you who are elderly, who feel the burden of the years. He loves those of you who are sick, those who are suffering from AIDS and from AIDS-related complex. He loves the relatives and friends of the sick and those who care for them. He loves us all with an unconditional and everlasting love.[66]

The bishops draw from a rich tradition regarding the common good as they approach the AIDS epidemic:

> Our understanding of the common good expresses our vision as a people of the kind of society we want to be. The common good is, therefore, central to the evaluation of legislative and public policy proposals. Two objectives are fundamental to any adequate understanding of the common good: first, preserving and protecting human dignity while guaranteeing the rights of all; second, caring for all who need help and cannot help themselves.[67]

In this communal vision, the individual's rights to privacy and liberty are balanced by that same individual's responsibility to avoid doing harm to others.

Consistent with their communitarian vision, the bishops state: "As members of the church and society, we have a responsibility to stand in solidarity with and reach out with compassion and understanding to those exposed or experiencing this disease."[68] They likewise "encourage all members of our society to relate to [AIDS] victims with compassion and understanding, as they would to those suffering from any other fatal disease."[69]

More specifically, the bishops' construction of AIDS condemns as "unjust and immoral" all forms of discrimination and violence against persons with AIDS and HIV[70] as well as the escalating violence directed specifically against gay and lesbian people in the wake of the epidemic.[71] They acknowledge the "unwarranted fear and undue alarm" in many communities as a result of inadequate education about how the virus is spread.[72] They list the specific "unconscionable deeds" resulting from that ignorance and fear: "the firebombing of a family's home because their sons had AIDS; the exclusion of students from school because they are infected with HIV; the isolation and virtual quarantining of other children in school situations; refusal by physicians and health-care workers to care for persons with AIDS; and assertions that a cure for AIDS will never be found because it is God's judgment on its victims."[73]

The bishops are quick to encourage Catholic hospitals to provide initiative and leadership in their work with persons with this disease. Likewise, with regard to Catholic schools, preschools, and agencies serving pregnant women, the bishops insist on making special accommodations in order to include those who are infected.

The bishops oppose "the enactment of quarantine legislation or other laws that are not supported by medical data or informed by the expertise of those in the health care or public health professions."[74] They likewise oppose the use of the HIV-antibody test for strictly discriminatory purposes.[75] The bishops insist that "persons with AIDS should be encouraged to lead productive lives in their community and place of work."[76]

At the same time, they also remind those already infected with the virus to take precautions to ensure that they do not expose anyone else to it. "If HIV-infected persons have rights which others must respect, they also must fulfill their fundamental ethical responsibility to avoid doing harm to others."[77]

To summarize what I have noted thus far, the Catholic human nature theory employed by the bishops places a strong emphasis on human community. In doing so, it stresses the rights of individuals to such necessities as protection, freedom, privacy, and basic economic security. It insists even further that a just society must give priority attention to those most in need. At the same time, this theory balances a concern for individual rights with individual responsibilities: the individual must avoid doing harm to others, must contribute to the common good. In this way, the Catholic theory of community strikes a careful balance between individual rights and the common good. It is thus able to account for many of the key values at stake in framing public policy on such thorny issues as confidentiality of HIV-test results, quarantining, mandatory testing, provision of adequate health care, and medical insurance.

Yet within the bishops' statements, another issue seems to be working itself out—namely, what is to be the relationship between the church and the larger pluralist American society? The bishops' construction of the AIDS epidemic is an instance in which this difficult issue within contemporary American Catholicism presents itself in bold relief.

When we compare the two statements, we can discern two very different approaches to this question. The first, as found in the USCC statement "The Many Faces of AIDS," is acutely sensitive to the plurality of cultures in American society. According to this approach, these other cultures, though often holding values very different from those in official Catholic teaching, are nevertheless as valid as American Catholicism itself. In the words of the Catholic social theorist John Courtney Murray, "Their validity in their own context and against the background of the history that generated them does not disturb [the Catholic] in his conviction that his own prejudice [i.e., judgments of value], within his own context and against the background of his own history, has its own validity."[78]

Consequently, the first document, while seeking to "offer a clear presentation of Catholic moral teaching," strives to do so in such a way as to respect the pluralism of values and attitudes in American society. "We speak as representatives of a religious tradition in a pluralistic society," this statement reads, "as, together with all persons of good will, we face the new and distinctive challenge of AIDS."[79] In this approach, moreover, the conclusions are deliberately tentative and the tone is clearly dialogical: "All that we say in this statement is not intended to be the last word on AIDS, but rather our contribution to the current dialogue."[80]

This first statement continues this clear and assertive, yet open-ended and dialogical, approach even when addressing the controversial issue of condoms. Thus, the bishops preface their discussion of condoms with "We speak to an entire nation, whose pluralism we recognize and respect."[81] They proceed to present guidelines for sex education programs reflecting the traditional Catholic sexual norms, but then follow that presentation with a reaffirmation of respect for the pluralistic character of the larger American society and the consequent need for dialogue:

> While we advocate the provision of more than mere biological information in sex education, we recognize that this raises important questions because of existing constitutional restraints or interpretations of the separation of church and state. We are willing to join other people of good

will in dialogue about how such a fuller understanding of human sexuality might be communicated in our public schools and elsewhere. We
believe that there are certain basic values present in our society which
transcend religious or sectarian boundaries and which can constitute a
common basis for these social efforts.[82]

In these words, the bishops are expressing confidence in the American
experience in which a plurality of distinct cultures has been able to find
common ground in certain shared moral assumptions. They also indicate their willingness to participate in that national experience on an
equal footing with those of other and diverse cultures.

It is at this point, having made the above affirmations, that the bishops delicately state what I quoted in the previous section, words that
later came to rankle conservative prelates:

Because we live in a pluralistic society, we acknowledge that some will
not agree with our understanding of human sexuality. We recognize that
public educational programs addressed to a wide audience will reflect the
fact that some people will not act as they can and should; that they will
not refrain from the type of sexual or drug abuse behavior which can
transmit AIDS. In such situations educational efforts, if grounded in the
broader moral vision outlined above, could include accurate information
about prophylactic devices or other practices proposed by some medical
experts as potential means of preventing AIDS. We are not promoting the
use of prophylactics, but merely providing information that is part of the
factual picture. Such a factual presentation should indicate that abstinence outside of marriage and fidelity within marriage as well as the
avoidance of intravenous drug abuse are the only morally correct and
medically sure ways to prevent the spread of AIDS.[83]

Clearly reflected in this statement is the desire to participate in pluralist
American society. Moreover, the bishops back up that desire with a
commitment to work with others in developing effective education programs:

In light of this position, as participants in the public life of this nation we
are willing to commit the best efforts of the U.S. Catholic Conference to
work on such programs. We also wish to assure legislators and public officials that we are willing to collaborate with them in the development of
an informed and enlightened public policy for the prevention of AIDS.[84]

In short, I believe it is possible to characterize this approach to the
church-in-a-pluralistic-society issue as characteristic of American Catholicism. At the same time that it clearly articulates the traditional ban

on prophylactics, it entertains a willingness to interact with other symbolic-moral universes on this topic. By taking this approach, the bishops seem to echo Murray's heartfelt hope for the nation as a whole:

> Perhaps the time has come when we should endeavor to dissolve the structure of war that underlies the pluralistic society, and erect the more civilized structure of the dialogue. It would be no less sharply pluralistic, but rather more so, since the real pluralisms would be clarified out of their present confusion. And amid the pluralism a unity would be discernible—the unity of an orderly conversation. The pattern would not be that of ignorant armies clashing by night but of informed men locked together in argument in the full light of a new dialectical day. Thus we might present to a "candid world" the spectacle of a civil society.[85]

By contrast, the bishops' second document, "Called to Compassion and Responsibility," rarely mentions the word "pluralism," and exhibits a different understanding of the church's role within the larger American culture. In this view, the church is to present moral teachings in more straightforward, unequivocal terms, with less room for dialogue. "[T]he use of prophylactics," as Cardinal O'Connor stated in his criticism of the first document, "is immoral in a pluralistic society or any other society."[86] Similarly, Cardinal Krol and Archbishop Bevilacqua reacted by stating that "our concern for others in a pluralistic society is best expressed in our persistent presentation of the church's moral principles and teaching."[87] There is less emphasis on dialogue here, and more emphasis on asserting the Catholic position in clear and forceful terms.

"Called to Compassion and Responsibility" reflects this latter view. It is distinct from the first statement not in the clarity with which it articulates the traditional Catholic sexual program, but in its lack of willingness to dialogue with other American cultures about that program's implications for the larger discourse on AIDS. For this reason, I perceive that the second statement fails to appreciate adequately the necessity and legitimacy of diversity within American society.

One final point is worth mentioning briefly. I stated above that our metaphors reflect the people with whom we are in dialogue. For this reason, it is worth noting that no recognized leaders of the gay community or people living with AIDS were invited to participate in drafting either of the two episcopal statements. While some gay individuals were perhaps part of the discussion, no official representatives of the Gay Men's Health Crisis, the San Francisco AIDS Foundation, the NAMES Project, or other significant AIDS organizations were invited to contribute. Unlike the federal government and the medical community, which have actively sought out gay and lesbian leaders from such highly respected AIDS agencies when drafting major legislation or developing treatment protocols, the American episcopal conference made no such efforts.[88]

Does the Metaphor Enable Individual PWAs to Live with Dignity, Determination, and Grace?

Metaphors for AIDS shape, for better or for worse, the ways in which people with AIDS come to view themselves, their illness, and the treatment they receive. Some metaphors empower people to approach AIDS with a certain gracefulness and determination to live fully and actively; other metaphors can cripple people with inappropriate anxiety, guilt, and alienation. The latter types of metaphor generally surround diseases that have become particularly stigmatized: those regarded as terminal, those linked to sexuality, those associated with already stigmatized groups, those that are grossly disfiguring, those for which there is no known cure, those believed to be contagious, and those whose natural histories remain unknown and mysterious.[89]

AIDS would likely have been stigmatized regardless of whom it first infected. A mysterious and terminal disease, often sexually transmitted, often disfiguring, presently incurable, feared by many to be contagious, AIDS would inevitably disrupt the stable identity of any given culture. It would forcefully confront the noninfected with the reality of death, assaulting what Alfred Schutz calls our "natural attitude," our construction of daily life in a way that minimizes or avoids the "fundamental anxiety."[90] Regardless of the groups that first became most directly affected by AIDS, we could have expected to find healthy persons searching for explanations that would clearly differentiate people with AIDS from themselves—differences as to biological predisposition perhaps, or behavioral idiosyncrasies. Moreover, as with other serious illnesses, people with AIDS would probably have been attributed with certain character flaws in a manner analogous to the characterization of cancer patients. (As Susan Sontag observes, cancer patients have often been blamed for their illness; e.g., they are viewed as repressing their emotions or lacking the will to live.[91]) In so doing, healthy persons could thereby distance themselves from death by defining as "other" those who carried this deadly disease. All of this would likely have occurred regardless of which people had first been hit by the epidemic.

But AIDS has, in fact, become a disease of groups that have already been stigmatized, frequently for their sexual expression. Therefore a double stigma is ascribed to it. A gay man with AIDS must deal with both the stigma of a disfiguring, terminal disease as well as with the inherited religious stigma so often attached to being a homosexual. As a result of the double stigma attached to AIDS, it becomes all the more difficult for a gay male PWA to live gracefully with his or her condition.

All of this becomes very real when, as is frequently the case, a gay man's disclosure of an AIDS diagnosis is also the moment when he first "comes out" to family and friends. The stress then becomes theirs as well. In such moments, as Gary Lloyd, a sociologist of the family, states: "Families with a member discovered to have HIV infection or diagnosed with AIDS will experience high levels of stress, and disruption in all areas of family life."[92]

This third criterion therefore attends to the effects of AIDS metaphors on PWAs themselves. It is clear that adequate metaphors for AIDS will be free of such stigmatizing elements as found in the "AIDS as divine punishment" metaphor and those that refer to other "innocent victims," i.e., those who did not contract the virus through sex or drugs. (In the words of one gay PWA: "Before it was known that AIDS was a transmittable virus, homosexuals like myself caught AIDS in what was very natural for us, the act of loving another man, a God-given gift to all of us homosexuals. We too are very innocent sufferers of AIDS."[93]) In short, adequate metaphors allow people with AIDS to live gracefully, without undue alienation, inappropriate guilt, paralyzing anxiety.

But the desire to avoid stigma must not lead us to another equally harmful extreme of reducing PWAs to mere medical cases, stripped of the particularities of their cultural identities in order to render them worthy of adequate care. Adequate understanding and treatment demands a sensitivity to people in their uniqueness and in the totality of their loves and relationships, rituals and customs. Sick people are not just sick people, as though part of a universal category lacking uniqueness and particularity. Rather, they are women and men with very particular significant others in their lives, unique cultural norms and traditions to which they adhere, specific work to which they have given themselves, distinct preferences in art and food and music. Such particularizing factors require acknowledgment and respect. This is true, of course, for all people who are sick, and it is equally so for PWAs who are gay or intravenous drug users. Metaphors that screen out such unique cultural factors with the supposedly benign intent of rendering an "impartial" understanding of the sick person's plight and treatment do more harm than good.

This is especially pertinent to the situation of PWAs and intravenous drug users whose cultural identities and kinship structures are more likely to be nonconventional in varying degrees. AIDS, in fact, has become a catalyst for redefining what we mean by the term "family." Carol Levine, executive director of New York City's Citizens Commission on AIDS, writes:

As more and more people live in nontraditional arrangements, the distance between their needs and interests and official designations widens. This discrepancy is apparent in many areas, but appears with particular force in AIDS, which, at the same time, heightens the summed impact and lays bare the multiple parts of dysfunctional designations and categories. Those most affected by AIDS and HIV infection—gay men, intravenous drug users and their sexual partners, largely from poor minority communities—are also those most likely to have nontraditional living or family arrangements. Even if they lived in traditional families before they became ill, the stigma of AIDS and the stress of coping with terminal illness may have created deep intrafamilial rifts. The person with AIDS may thus have to acquire a new family for emotional and economic support.[94]

Not to acknowledge and respect the unique cultural and family structures of many PWAs is to overlook a critical piece of the PWA's experience as she or he copes with this illness.

Thus, adequate metaphors for AIDS must not only avoid stigmatizing people with this disease but must also acknowledge and respect the diverse cultural identities of PWAs, the validity of their family structures and support networks, their symbols and values and rituals. (As is true whenever we are attending to cultures other than our own, such acknowledgment and respect do not necessarily have to mean total agreement.)

Perhaps a scene from the movie *Gandhi* illustrates the posture I am proposing here. Throughout the story, Gandhi is struggling to bring to an end the bitter war between the Muslims and the Hindus. In one poignant scene, a Hindu leader comes to the bedside of Gandhi, who, at this point, is weak from several days of fasting. The Hindu tells him that the Muslims have captured and killed his son. He goes on to say that he, in retaliation, has captured a Muslim boy and done the same to him. Then, in agony, he concludes: "I am going to hell." As Gandhi looks at the man, he whispers: "I think I know a way out of hell." He tells the man to go into the Muslim section of the city and find there a boy, about the same age as his son who had been killed, a boy who has been left homeless and without family as a result of the war. He counsels him: "Bring him into your home as your own son, *and raise him as a Muslim.*" In a worldview such as Gandhi's it is possible for two radically different cultures to honor and respect each other. Such an expansive worldview is needed today as we come to terms with this epidemic.

Finally, this third criterion requires us to take seriously questions of ultimate meaning. AIDS, like so many other human tragedies, elicits the inevitable questions "Why? Why me? Why this group of people? Why now?" In a post-Enlightenment Western culture, such questions are all too cavalierly brushed aside.[95] Yet Western scientific rationality alone cannot "get at" the struggle underlying such questions, a struggle simply to make sense out of human tragedy. Sociologist Robert Bellah tells the story of an interview conducted by one of his colleagues. The interview was with an expert at the Environmental Protection Agency, and it had to do with how that agency figures the tradeoffs in the costs of human lives saved versus the costs of safety devices that would save them. The interviewer suggested: "Some people believe human life is priceless." The government expert replied, "We have no data on that."[96] There are some crucial issues of an ultimate nature, such as the value to be placed on human life, that scientific calculation alone cannot address.

So it is with the ultimate questions we find ourselves asking when confronted with the death of young people in the present AIDS crisis. These questions cannot be answered with even the most up-to-date biomedical information. Rather, they require responsible art and ritual and theology. AIDS metaphors must respect the basic human need to grapple honestly with such ultimate questions.

We turn, then, to the construction of AIDS by the American Catholic bishops. Clearly their concern as spiritual and pastoral leaders is to find within the Christian and Catholic mythos a place for the experience of AIDS, one that will give it an ultimate meaning. They derive from the vision and teaching of Jesus a metaphor for the way we ourselves might view AIDS:

> One of the distinctive aspects of Jesus' ministry was the manner in which he took the common and not-so-common events of human life and revealed a meaning or potentiality that most, if not all, of his contemporaries had not discovered: that human love is revelatory of divine love, that death can disclose the possibility of new life. The challenge facing today's followers of the risen Lord is to do the same with contemporary experiences, whether of joy or sorrow, to discover the deeper meaning that might otherwise remain hidden.

One such experience is the presence of AIDS in our country and other parts of the world.[97]

They show their pastoral sensitivity to the various dimensions of that struggle to find meaning:

> Persons with AIDS, their families and their friends need solidarity, comfort and support. As with others facing imminent death, they may experience anger toward and alienation from God and the church as they face the inevitability of dying. It is important that someone stand with them in their pain and help them, in accord with their religious tradition, to discover meaning in what appears so meaningless.[98]

They draw upon a rich spiritual tradition that regards human suffering as redemptive, an opportunity for growth that finally culminates in the fuller and more abundant life of resurrection. They quote the encyclical *Salvifici Doloris* with its metaphor for suffering as an act of giving birth:

> In the messianic program of Christ, which is at the same time the program of the kingdom of God, suffering is present in the world in order to release love, in order to give birth to works of love toward neighbor, in order to transform the whole of human civilization into a "civilization of love."[99]

The bishops are careful to overcome the stigma associated with AIDS. They explicitly reject the idea that this illness is a direct punishment by God, and they assert that "God is compassionate, not vengeful."[100] As I mentioned earlier, they are careful to overcome the portrayal of PWAs as "other," and they explicitly condemn violence against PWAs, and against lesbians and gay men. They call for education programs that can alleviate fear, prejudice, and discrimination against PWAs. Mindful of their own responsibility to educate pastoral caregivers, they ask every diocese to develop training programs for those who minister to people affected by AIDS or ARC.[101] They likewise "call upon each diocese to appoint, where appropriate, a person responsible for coordinating its ministry to persons with AIDS and their loved ones."[102]

When they set out to articulate the moral norms that should govern sexual and other behavior throughout this crisis, they are careful to state that their intention is not to increase the stigma already attached to the disease. Rather, "the primary concern of our observations is people's moral and physical well-being, not their condemnation, however much

we might disagree with their actions."[103] Disagreement, in their view, is
not meant to imply condemnation. In sum, they assert:

> For Christians, then, stories of persons with AIDS must not become occa-
> sions for stereotyping or prejudice, for anger or recrimination, for rejec-
> tion or isolation, for injustice or condemnation. They provide us with an
> opportunity to walk with those who are suffering, to be compassionate to-
> ward those whom we might otherwise fear, to bring strength and courage
> both to those who face the prospect of dying as well as to their loved
> ones.[104]

Yet it appears that their desire to offer compassion and support, their
effort to counter the stigma attached to AIDS, chafes against their
equally sincere desire, described earlier, to reaffirm the traditional Catholic sexual code: "As bishops, we must offer a clear presentation of
Catholic moral teaching concerning human intimacy and sexuality."[105]

A metaphor the bishops invoke in both statements to describe the relationships between the church and the person with AIDS is Jesus' story
of the prodigal son. In that powerful story, the son "discovered that the
way he had chosen, the way of sin, was leading him to death. His very
life hung on the choice to return to his father."[106] This repentant prodigal
son is then welcomed joyfully by the father, analogous to the way the
church is now called upon to welcome those persons with AIDS who,
repentant, now seek the church's assistance.

The problem is, what should be done with those self-affirming gay
PWAs who, though not repentant, still seek out the church's assistance?
Father Xavier John Seubert tells of an encounter with one such person, a
gay man with AIDS whom he visited before the man died.

> At one point, this person called and asked me to come to his apartment so
> that he could receive Eucharist for Easter. I went and we talked for a
> while. Before beginning our ritual, I asked him if he wanted to receive the
> sacrament of reconciliation. He thought for a moment and then said to
> me: "I am homosexual, and that is that. I am very sick and that is that. I
> am going to die soon, and that is that. I have a deep relationship to Jesus
> and it is a great consolation to me. And that is that! No, I have no need of
> confession."[107]

Prescinding for a moment from the pastoral dimensions of this particular situation, I want to call attention to the official posture of the American bishops. This posture has been, I believe, correctly summarized by
Chicago's archbishop, Cardinal Bernardin:

From a moral point of view, we do not approve of certain sexual activities through which AIDS can be transmitted, and we must be very clear about encouraging people to live in accordance with the church's moral code. We teach what is morally right and wrong. But when a person has AIDS, then we are nonjudgmental. The person may or may not have contracted the disease through an immoral action of behavior. We treat AIDS as a human disease, and we reach out to the person with compassion. We do not ask how he or she contracted the disease.[108]

The first of the episcopal statements perhaps capsulizes the resulting position vis-à-vis those PWAs who remain "unrepentant" in the eyes of the church: "[W]e encourage all members of our society to relate to [AIDS] victims with compassion and understanding, *as they would to those suffering from any other fatal disease* [my emphasis]."[109] This construction of the person with AIDS has much to offer that is positive. It allows for the compassionate care of PWAs, regardless of how they contracted the disease, regardless of whether they are in the good graces of the official church. I believe, however, that it is inadequate to the degree that it disencumbers the individual PWA of his or her unique cultural identity, failing to respect the relationships, values, and symbols that have given meaning to that person's life. Perhaps, in at least this respect, the worldview of Gandhi is more expansive, and therefore more adequate, than that currently offered by the American bishops.

The Bishops' Metaphors for AIDS

I have suggested three criteria by which to measure the adequacy of AIDS metaphors: such metaphors empower us in our efforts to end the epidemic, contribute to social cohesiveness, and enable PWAs to live with dignity, determination, and grace. In applying these same criteria to the American Catholic bishops' constructions of AIDS, I have tried to point out the ways in which I find those constructions to be adequate, drawing as they do from a rich tradition that emphasizes such values as justice and compassion, a respect for modern science, the rights of the individual as well as the common good, the value of human life as well as of human suffering and death. I have also tried to point out the areas in which I have found their current constructions of AIDS to be inadequate, and this has been largely in their concern within the present epidemic to reassert the rather narrow metaphors of the Catholic sexual program and their unwillingness to dialogue with and respect other voices in the larger American culture, particularly the gay community.

To stop at this point, however, would give a very lopsided view of the American Catholic construction of AIDS. For the majority of Catholics, religious metaphors are often less a matter of hierarchical statements and more a matter of run-of-the-mill encounters with a nun, a parish priest, or a lay minister. We turn now, therefore, to examine the ways in which Catholic pastoral caregivers working within this epidemic have defined its meaning for themselves and those for whom they care.

4 The Challenges of Catholic AIDS Ministry: Conversations with Pastoral Caregivers

The American Catholic church, like much of American culture, is struggling with the question of what AIDS means. As we saw in chapter 3, the American hierarchy has drawn upon the Catholic tradition of social justice and a rich repertoire of myths, symbols, and rituals in constructing the meaning it ascribes to this disease. At the same time, unlike the process they employed when formulating their pastoral statements on the economy or the question of nuclear war, the bishops did not formally dialogue with gay leaders as they developed their construction of AIDS. Not only did the bishops not consult such highly respected national organizations as New York's Gay Men's Health Crisis or the San Francisco AIDS Foundation, they even further distanced themselves from the gay community by using the epidemic as an occasion in which to reaffirm the traditional anti-homosexual ethic and to forbid the use of condoms as a prophylaxis in preventing the spread of the disease. The result is a mixed message—calls for compassion and social justice for PWAs issued simultaneously with condemnations of the values of one of the groups most influential in the larger American AIDS discourse—that has compromised the American hierarchy's ability to participate credibly in the larger American discourse on AIDS.

Yet the American hierarchy's construction of the AIDS epidemic cannot necessarily be said to represent those of other sectors of the American church. Like so much of American culture at large, the American Catholic church shares in the current polarization between orthodox and progressive viewpoints. In this polarized situation, other voices vie with those of the bishops in seeking to make some sense out of this tragedy. The voices that prevail will, in the end, decide what AIDS means from a Catholic standpoint.

In this chapter I am going to look at another important voice within this pluriform American Catholic community, namely, that of Catholic pastoral caregivers. Specifically, I want to describe and summarize a number of conversations I have had with eighteen such ministers. Whether they hold highly visible positions within a chancery office or work quietly at the bedsides of those dying from the disease, these men and women could be said to represent an even more powerful voice than that of the bishops. They are what the Italian theorist Antonio Gramsci referred to as the "organic intellectuals" who perform an essential mediating function in the clash of conflicting social groups,[1] in this case, between PWAs who generally represent marginalized cultures on the one hand, and the American Catholic hierarchy on the other.

According to Gramsci, during periods of social transformation, traditional and progressive forces rival each other, and the outcome of their rivalry results in either the restoration of the old cultural hegemony or the establishment of a new one. In order for either side to prevail, it is not enough simply for the ruling authority to exercise political power, since a cultural hegemony cannot simply be imposed through sheer domination. A true cultural hegemony also requires the ability to elicit "spontaneous consent" from the majority of groups in society through the exercise of genuine leadership that is credible in the eyes of people representing a broad range of interests and social viewpoints. It is here, in Gramsci's view, that the necessary role of the intellectual becomes apparent. It is the intellectual's job to provide the necessary leadership, and this means serving as the link between those in power and the social masses. Gramsci thus spoke of two types of intellectuals: those he called "traditional," who present themselves as heirs of the truths of the past, and those he called "organic," who, while familiar with the traditional worldview, represent new voices calling for reform. If the organic intellectuals are to succeed in establishing a new cultural hegemony, they must find a way to assimilate the traditional vision through conversation and compromise. Hence the need for organic intellectuals to be conversant with both the traditional worldview in order to transform it as well as with the reformist worldview they represent. The effectiveness of these intellectuals is a critical factor in deciding which side of the cultural conflict will finally prevail.

The men and women described in this chapter are organic intellectuals within the American Catholic community. Their constructions of this epidemic are identifiably Catholic, yet significantly different from those found in the official hierarchical statements. As organic intellectuals, their experiences and their ability (or failure) to achieve influence in the larger discussion of AIDS will profoundly shape—for better or for worse—the way in which the American Catholic church comes to construct this disease.

The ministers described in this chapter do not constitute a random sample as one might find in more standard sociological surveys.[2] I did my research in two major archdioceses, one on the West Coast and one in the Midwest. When I arrived in each archdiocese, I spent several hours informally asking around through the local Catholic and gay grapevines in an effort to identify the leaders among ministers in the Catholic AIDS ministry. Those whose names surfaced most frequently and consistently were the ones I chose to interview. I believe that I was able to identify most, though not all, of the leading AIDS ministers in the two archdioceses I surveyed, and I am willing to suggest that the group of people I finally selected do in fact represent a significant portion of American Catholic AIDS ministers.

No efforts were made on my part to be neutral or "objective" in the course of these interviews. I was not in search of "pure data." Rather, I was an active participant in each interview, seeking to explore with each minister the journey he or she had undertaken and the ways in which each gave shape and meaning to that journey. At times I found myself merely listening attentively as they spoke. At other times I found myself more actively probing their statements, pushing for greater elaboration and clarity. Although I tried to be a good listener, I made no effort to be dispassionate about or detached from what I was hearing.[3]

In seeking to discover how these women and men fulfill their roles as organic intellectuals, I focused my questions to them in two directions. First of all, I asked very practical questions, such as "Who pays your salary?" and "To whom are you accountable in your job?" Through such questions I tried to learn how these ministers have positioned themselves, in practical terms, vis-à-vis the institutional church. Second, I asked questions concerning their perceptions and constructions of themselves, the individuals they serve, and the epidemic as a whole. I asked, for example, what each of them might want to say to the pope about what they have learned from their pastoral experience in this epidemic. I asked them to describe for me how they understand AIDS from a theological standpoint. I asked them to imagine bringing together all of the people with whom they have come into contact during the course of their AIDS ministry, and then to imagine what they might want to say to such a gathering. Most of all, I asked them simply to tell me stories —stories about their own journey into this critical and sometimes controversial ministry, and stories about the people they serve and with whom they work. Through such questions, I was hoping to discover the norms and values, the symbols and myths and rituals from which they drew in interpreting their experiences.

Since I am working within the theoretical framework that says that we human beings fashion our perceptions of ourselves and the world out of our interaction with the cultures around us, I understand that these ministers fashion a significant part of their professional and personal perceptions out of their interaction with (1) the gay community, and (2) the American Catholic community. I am suggesting that it is the nature of these cultures and the quality of interaction of these ministers with them that significantly determine how these ministers view themselves, how they construct their personal and professional identities, and how they construct the epidemic in which they work.

There are two extremes to avoid when interacting with another culture. The first extreme is to shield oneself from a genuine understanding of the other culture and from any changes that such interaction might require. In this instance, one opts so vigorously for the continuity of one's prior identity that true interaction with the other culture cannot occur. The other extreme is to opt so vigorously for the other culture, for change, that one loses continuity with one's own prior identity, traditions, and roots. The danger here is the disintegration of one's existing identity structure. Between these two extremes lies a necessary balance: one remains faithful to his or her prior identity, yet fully and genuinely interacts with the other culture, understanding it adequately and adapting to it when appropriate. The history of the church is replete with examples of this balanced interaction, as is evidenced, for example, in the incorporation of so many pagan symbols and rituals (e.g., the Christmas tree, many elements of the Easter liturgy, popular beliefs concerning Purgatory, miracles, and saints) into an ongoing Christian belief and practice.

It is in balancing these two cultures that the men and women in this chapter reveal themselves to be organic intellectuals. They provide the necessary link between two cultures vying for hegemony in the American Catholic discourse on AIDS—namely, on the one side, those voices within the American church that tend to be more sympathetic to the gay community and, on the other side, the more conservative elements of the American Catholic hierarchy. Thus, these men and women are themselves organically rooted in and profoundly shaped by the gay community, its experiences of oppression, its aspirations for liberation, and its symbols, values, and ethical norms. On the other hand, these ministers, as we will see, are knowledgeable of and fully conversant with the official and traditional teachings of the hierarchy—as they must be if they are to maintain an identity as official representatives of the church. They are thus located in the interstices of two conflicting cultures, seeking to strike a balance that is as delicate as it is crucial in the ongoing construction of AIDS.

How have these women and men exercised their role as organic intellectuals? How have they fared when it comes to striking the important balance between maintaining a genuine Catholic identity and the need to take seriously the emerging gay culture? Most important, how have they come to understand this epidemic: What meaning, in their minds, does it hold? An examination of their stories may provide not only some insight into the evolving Catholic construction of AIDS, but may also shed some light on the interactions of other American Catholics within contemporary American culture.

Interactions with the Gay Community

I would regard all the men and women I spoke with as "gay-positive," that is, as regarding homosexuality as a normal variant of human sexuality in general. While maintaining some critical perspectives on gay culture, they nevertheless understand being gay as a legitimate and healthy sexual identity. They also seem to feel relatively comfortable when interacting with members of the gay community, if not on a social level, then at least on a professional level in order to address the pastoral and other exigencies of the epidemic.

This empathy with the gay community, as we will see, has led these ministers to convictions different from those of the bishops. Unlike the bishops, they are *not* of the opinion that AIDS results from immoral behavior. They do not see its remedy as a simple return to a traditional sexual ethic. Moreover, they do not find it necessary, as they provide the rationale for their ministry, benignly to disregard the fact that a given client might be gay and in a relationship with a person of the same sex; on the contrary, they see such relationships as calling for affirmation and respect. In these ways, these ministers are operating from a worldview that is different from that of the bishops. Consequently, as we will see in more detail, their construction of AIDS is noticeably different as well.

One wife and mother began her AIDS ministry after becoming sensitized to the religious and spiritual needs of her own gay son and those of other gay men and women. A parish minister for fifteen years, she had become increasingly disappointed with the church's response to AIDS. "It was such an antiseptic response," she said, "focused on how to keep from contracting and spreading the virus rather than on working with the people who had it." She looked for alternative ways of doing AIDS ministry that would be less alienating to gay men. Her search eventually led her into a pastoral training program geared specifically to the needs of PWAs at a large, urban, non-Catholic hospital.

Perhaps not surprisingly, many of the ministers I interviewed told me that they are themselves gay. These ministers frequently had moved into AIDS ministry as an extension of their prior ministry within the gay community. One gay priest, for example, told me that his involvement in AIDS work had flowed out of his previous ministry with a gay prayer group. After a member of that group, a hospital worker, had come across a gay man with AIDS dying alone, the prayer group was able to connect with the dying man, providing support and keeping vigil in his final days and hours. As a result of that experience, this priest called the local AIDS foundation and requested training to work within the epidemic.

As previously occurred in the psychiatric community when psychiatrists and mental health professionals interacted with the gay community, the interaction of these ministers with the gay community has had an impact on how they have come to construct homosexuality itself. Many of the ministers mentioned how they have changed, coming to view homosexuality in more positive terms as a result of their interaction with gay men in the course of the epidemic. The story of one openly gay minister, a former Jesuit seminarian, illustrates the type of reconstruction of homosexuality that can occur.

When this man was first coming out of the closet in the mid-1980s, but before he had come to know many openly gay people, AIDS had already become part of the gay landscape. While still a Jesuit, he became aware of the efforts of one archdiocese to set up its own ministry for PWAs, and he spent two months during a summer working in that effort, often shoulder to shoulder with other gay men.

> That experience changed me as a gay person in the church and in other ways. I saw other gay men who were responsible, with a social perspective that didn't match the broader cultural perspective of gay men. Generativity was operative in a very real way. I met one person involved in this epidemic who had ARC and he was helping other people while dealing with his own stuff. This experience helped me to see that God might be here as well as other places.

After leaving the Jesuits, this man eventually took a position as a director of a large service agency attached to a parish. "I've grown a lot personally,'' he told me, ''and I've seen a depth of character and compassion I wouldn't have experienced otherwise. When I look for God in the world, I continue to look for God in the midst of this.''

For yet another minister, a nun now working with disadvantaged youth, the encounter with gay men came after a journey in which she, as a graduate student in theology, first began questioning the Catholic sexual ethic from the perspective of the women's movement. ''I became aware of lots of questions,'' she said, and then added jokingly, ''I began to wonder if I had any ethics at all!'' This general questioning of the Catholic sexual ethic opened her up to the struggles of specific groups within the church, including gay men and lesbians, concerning that same ethic. This openness in turn led her to seek training in pastoral ministry geared to PWAs, most of whom were gay men. The consequent exposure to gay men through her pastoral work in the epidemic shed a different light on her understanding of homosexuality and of her own heterosexuality as well.

I am not homosexual, so going into AIDS ministry was going into a world that was not part of my experience. I went in as a student. I knew some things, but I didn't know what it means to be a homosexual person. They taught me what it means to be a gay man in this city and in this country. I grew in my own level of sexual understanding of myself and of comfort with corners of my own life that I had held at bay. Otherwise I don't think I'd be very comfortable doing the work I'm doing now with kids on the street. I learned a lot about what relationship means, because I saw it in ways I had not previously seen before in my life. I learned other ways of understanding family, and how to offer support within that family/friend network, how to be pastor for a different kind of family. I really wish the heterosexual community, especially heterosexual men, would lighten up and be more open and learn from the gay community. Because with a gay couple, they both have to do everything in the household. A lot of heterosexual men probably could learn something. I saw a lot of love and it was good to bear witness to it and be able to tell that story.

A number of the ministers I interviewed referred to what they regarded as a genuine moral growth that had occurred within the gay culture as a result of its experience of AIDS.

I've seen the way people have transcended their own needs and pettiness: after spending eight to ten hours in their own jobs, they'll spend three or four hours helping someone with HIV. I've also seen the ways people have changed their behaviors around something as basic as sexuality— not only to protect themselves but other people as well—a transcendence of self. I believe that God's spirit is present in all those things.

As a result of their experiences of working in the gay community during this epidemic, these men and women have come to question the official, more traditional construction of homosexuality within the American Catholic church. Most of the ministers with whom I spoke already had come to regard the Catholic sexual ethic as inadequate even before they began their AIDS ministry. Most of them further sharpened their critique of that ethic as a result of wrestling with the exigencies of the epidemic. One minister stated it this way:

> AIDS has opened a door between gay people and the church. It gives a lot of people in the church an excuse, a safe avenue to work in the gay community without being labeled. AIDS has been an agent prompting reflection on sexuality. It's brought a lot of priests out of the closet. Working in the gay community has not been the big bugaboo they feared. They see heroism and selfless activity in the gay community. They come to ask: How could this be bad? How could this be what the church is telling us it is?

This interaction with the gay community, and the reconstruction of homosexuality it has generated in these ministers, stands in marked contrast to the unwillingness of many members of the American hierarchy to have any dialogue with the gay community whatsoever. Many of these ministers expressed to me their rage and sadness at the apparent unwillingness of the hierarchy to take seriously the lived experience of people in the gay and lesbian communities. One priest, when asked if there was anything he would want to convey to the pope about his experience working in the epidemic, put it this way:

> I could put my message into one word: Listen. Listen to people's stories so that we can discover the sacred in them. The difficulty I have with the church and the hierarchy is a positive inability to listen to people's stories, so they're not dealing with a movement I believe to be of God's spirit.

Another minister, a woman working in a shelter for homeless PWAs, expressed anger regarding Catholic teaching on homosexuality in these words:

> The church is terrible at addressing this issue internally, so how can it ever do it externally? I don't know who's going to be the prod for that. I have a sense it may be the laity, because we've given the clergy long enough, and they've done a terrible job of it. It's a frightening can of worms to open, but until it happens we're all going to continue to act as if there's nothing wrong. This huge issue stares everybody in the face, and

yet we turn as if it's not a problem at all. I find it kind of scary. I sense there are a lot of us who are fed up with this.

Another minister, a community health nurse concerned about education to prevent the spread of HIV, stated:

I'm a community health nurse; prevention is the key. But you can only have prevention if you have decent education. So very much a piece of that, as far as AIDS is concerned, is that you have to have a base there of a really good education on homosexuality. We missed the boat. We've got the rules, but we don't have any understanding of sexuality.

Yet another minister stated:

There are extraordinary circumstances when we have to ask whether our rules and principles, our moral framework, are really serving us. HIV is not affecting just gay men in this city, but people in Miami and Harlem and Ohio and Spokane, and it's endemic in Nairobi and Bangkok. This is an extraordinary time, and our moral framework—the basic principles governing sexual conduct and how we include some communities more easily than our own—is not serving us well.

These ministers I have just cited share a conviction I observed in all of the Catholic AIDS ministers I interviewed: The traditional sexual ethic is inadequate and has tragic consequences when viewed from the standpoint of this epidemic.

As a result of their interaction with the gay community, some of the ministers with whom I spoke felt that the church's credibility around AIDS was clearly undermined in the gay community by the inadequacy of its official construction of homosexuality. One individual, a member of Dignity, when asked what he thought the local bishop could do to assist in ending the epidemic, replied:

Perform a marriage ceremony for two gay people who love each other, or don't even bother addressing the issue of AIDS. You just can't minister to a community that you don't approve of. You can't extend the hand of hospitality while slapping them with the other hand. People aren't stupid.

This tension between the hierarchy and the gay community has made it difficult for many of the ministers I spoke with to establish trust and a professional rapport with elements of the gay community. In some instances the difficulty was ascribed to an anti-Catholic sentiment within the gay community; in other instances it was attributed to an incoherent AIDS policy on the part of the church. One minister mentioned that local gay newspapers had been quick to note whenever problems would

occur in his agency's programs, sometimes distorting the facts through
an anti-Catholic lens. Another minister mentioned the stigma she felt
both as a Catholic and as a woman when working with other AIDS
agencies composed largely of gay men who had become hostile to the
church. Trying to give a credible explanation of the problematic position of the hierarchy proved all the more challenging in such contexts.

> Once in a while if someone is willing to listen and knows the Catholic
> theological system, I'll try to explain—using the bishops' first document
> as my guideline—that we can speak of condoms in a pluralistic society.
> Unfortunately, it all sounds like doublespeak to someone who is really
> challenging the church's position. It *is* doublespeak. Other church leaders
> with whom I've worked in national efforts have acknowledged that it's
> doublespeak, too.

This effort to establish trust with the gay community has often required these ministers to downplay their connection to the institutional
church when speaking to gay individuals or groups. The director of a
Catholic Charities AIDS service, for instance, stated that, when relating
to gay organizations, he prefers to emphasize the structural separation
between his agency and the archdiocese, even though the former remains legally under the direction of the archbishop.

Yet, despite the obstacles in relating to the gay community, these
men and women could recount many instances in which an initial antip-
athy on the part of gay leaders had been softened. One minister was able
to list several programs in which hundreds of volunteers have been re-
cruited from Catholic parishes to provide practical and emotional support to PWAs and their loved ones. He described a newly emerging picture of church people in the minds of gay AIDS activists, a picture he
summarized as: "Church people are good. They just need to be asked."

This minister, moreover, told me the story of his struggle to head off
a major riot, called for by a national gay leader, at one of the international AIDS conferences. He and his agency had been among the early
ones, religious or otherwise, to publicly challenge the gay leader's call.
As a result, when he attended a meeting of ACT UP, he was personally
attacked for being yet another Catholic official obstructing that group's
demands for fair and effective medical and governmental responses to
the epidemic. Fortunately, the ensuing exchange led not to increased
hostility, but to a strategy session that in turn resulted in a large
nonviolent demonstration uniting ACT UP members and professional
participants at the conference. Alliances became forged, and a mutual
respect established between AIDS activists, medical professionals, and

pastoral ministers. The activists came to see him and his agency as genuinely concerned people and allies in the battle against AIDS.

Thus, in the interaction between these ministers and the gay community, the ministers have not been the only ones who have changed their
minds. Members of the gay community, in their exchanges with these
ministers, found themselves discarding some of their own stereotypes of
Catholics and Catholic institutions.

These ministers, then, have come to construct AIDS out of their own
direct involvement with the gay community—an involvement that, despite its tensions and struggles, has been positive and empathetic. Pre-
dictably, then, they do not view this disease as the natural result of
departing from traditional sexual norms. Rather, as one minister in a
shelter for homeless PWAs put it, "AIDS is not something that comes
from God, but God certainly stands before us in a very special way in
the faces of the people that we minister to, persons who come through
these doors." Another minister, relying on both biomedical data as well
as the Gospel, interpreted the disease in these words:

> AIDS is a disease, like cancer. People get it through sexual contact. Some
> sexual contact is promiscuous, unhealthy—but not necessarily in my
> mind. God loves us and made us. Gay people are gay. I didn't choose to
> be gay—it's too painful to choose it because it's not accepted. But God
> loves me. If someone has abused drugs or been a prostitute, the Gospel is
> there telling us not to judge.

Like many mental health professionals, these ministers regard homosexuality as a normal variant of human sexuality in general. Their positive view of homosexuality has been reinforced in their experience of
working within the epidemic, for in their contact with the gay community, these ministers have come to see much growth, heroism, and self-
lessness. They have also, in many instances, come to win the admiration
of many leaders in the gay and AIDS communities. Consequently, these
ministers do not view AIDS as an effect of sexual immorality, as official
statements from the hierarchy have sometimes implied. Moreover, as
we will see more fully later, they are able to embrace gay PWAs with all
their relationships and the many values, symbols, rituals, and institutions that shape their gay identity. In their view, the remedy for the
epidemic is not a return to the traditional sexual ethic, nor is it always
abstinence. The remedy, rather, lies in safer sex and adequate education,
which they are willing to promote, but, as we shall see, with varying degrees of candor and forthrightness.

Leaving the Church

This interaction with the gay community led one of these eighteen ministers to leave both the ministry and the Catholic church in order to embrace what could be termed an emerging gay religious consciousness. His story raises some interesting issues for American Catholicism.

A former superior in his religious community, he had been missioned to found and direct a resource center for PWAs in a poor and racially mixed neighborhood. Later, he left the church, in part because he became frustrated with its unwillingness to invest enough of its own resources in responding to the epidemic. After his departure, he achieved a master's degree in order to become a counselor, a role he has now assumed in a large nonprofit agency in a major city. In reviewing the church's track record on AIDS, this man said:

> I feel AIDS is an opportunity that has been missed. I don't find the church very involved in AIDS work. Catholic Charities here in this city does all its own grant-writing, and is therefore funded by nonchurch sources. They're not getting money to do that [i.e., AIDS work] from the church itself. Their services are administered under a Catholic umbrella, but it's not like the archdiocese is doing much in making this happen. I just don't find a whole lot changing. I find most of their efforts pitiful.

Perhaps more significant for this man was his experience of weariness from trying, in the context of an AIDS ministry, to walk the line between two communities in conflict.

> For many Catholics, going into AIDS work has been a revitalizing experience of their faith. And it was to me in some ways. But ultimately it led me out because it couldn't be sustained, not with the church holding the positions that it does and being so hostile to the gay community. The inconsistencies of their stand get to be too much for some of us to deal with. For years I walked this very strange line between the gay community, which was primarily the group affected by AIDS in the early days, and the church, and somehow I could justify that. But I think I finally stopped feeling I had to justify it. The inconsistency of having these men who were so out of touch with my experience, who didn't seem interested, simply got to be too much. The more I saw them drift to the right and into the security of dogma and tradition, I knew they weren't listening to whatever the spirit was saying through this experience. I don't feel it's my duty to enlighten them if they don't want it.

This minister came to reject his Catholic affiliation as dysfunctional for himself and other gay men.

My greatest difficulty is with gay men who keep going back to that church. I don't know how they can go near that church and worship. It blows my mind. I try not to judge them or let it interfere with people who do use that. But the only analogy I have is the abused or battered child that keeps going back to the parent that abused them. There's a security there, the knowledge that this is the only parent I have.

This man concluded that the vehicles many Catholics have used to make sense out of their lives "are just not working anymore." So he left the ministry and the church.

The alternative to Catholicism that he has chosen for himself, and proposes to other gay men, is in what he calls a "gay spirit," a unique spirituality and worldview that he is confident exists and is only now being rediscovered. This gay spirituality, he acknowledges, is still emerging and still somewhat vague. Yet, in his mind, it constitutes a viable religious cosmology, one that stands as an alternative to mainline organized religions.

I think we should go back and look again at what has set us [gay men] apart throughout history. And I think that's a sense of a gay spirit that has been degraded and ignored and is really just emerging. It's coming up because it can't be suppressed any longer. And AIDS is one of the vehicles that it's emerging through. Harry Hay, the founder of the modern gay movement, talks about the language, a way of believing, a faith system that has nothing to do with traditional Judeo-Christian values or any other organized religions. I don't think any of us know what it all means yet, but it's going back and finding out what those roots are all about. One of the roots of gay men throughout history has been our roles as healers and teachers and artists and shamans. I think there's just so much there that we don't understand fully and I'm not very clear about this even now. We will become more conscious of it as we uncover it and go deeper into this experience of so much death, so much loss. Through these kinds of holocaust, you do go deeper and you do look again at everything you take for granted. I'm not so sure the answers are going to be the ones we expect.

Such words may indicate the discovery (or perhaps the genesis) of a uniquely gay religion.

Whether a gay religion and a corresponding "gay spirit" can actually be traced throughout history as this man suggests is a debatable point among scholars. Nevertheless, as I stated in chapter 2, a bona fide gay culture is certainly emerging in the contemporary American scene. Within this former minister's stated experience, this culture possesses an explicitly religious element, a gay "sacred canopy" to rival that of

Catholicism. It could be said, correctly, I believe, that this man underwent a religious conversion in choosing to identify religiously as a gay man rather than as a Catholic. Yet his conversion did not appear to be a cut-and-dried affair. Ironically, his American Catholic heritage remained apparent in the values he presented, and the language he used to describe his experience. It also became apparent in his tone of voice and the passion with which he spoke of the church. For he did not speak of the church as though he were a disinterested bystander. He spoke, rather, as someone with strong convictions about what the church should be, and with feelings of anger, sadness, and betrayal as a result of what he viewed as the church's failure to adequately respond to gay people and PWAs.

From a theological point of view, this man's worldview is a post–Vatican II theological heritage, one that eschews rigid hierarchy and closed dogma, valuing openness to the Spirit as it moves among the people of God and in the world. It is likewise a progressive American heritage that values democracy and dialogue among church members and between church and world. It is out of this worldview of a progressive American Catholic that he critiques Catholicism itself.

> I would say to the pope, "You can't hear what the Spirit's saying to you. You're missing it, and I don't know what's going to open you up." I used to think that all these priests and brothers getting AIDS might open the hierarchy. I don't think it is. I see them even more closed than they were a few years ago. It's the same with all the sexual issues; they've barricaded themselves in, whether it is pedophilia, divorce, premarital sex. I don't think they have anything to say because they refuse to listen to the spirit as it's speaking through the people. I'd say to the pope . . . I don't know how I could find anything to say that would be dramatic enough. I often think of that piece of scripture about the only sin that can't be forgiven is the sin against the Holy Spirit. I don't know what that sin is, but I've often thought it was closing your heart off to the voice of the Holy Spirit. I think the church has done that. They're not listening to the Spirit anymore. They're listening to each other in that very rarefied atmosphere of hierarchy. I don't think they're listening to the Spirit as it speaks in many other forms.

Thus, this man's interaction with others in the gay culture had evolved, in part, out of his American and post–Vatican II worldview. It was, in his view, a matter of attentiveness to the Spirit of God moving in the world. His exit from the church grew out of his concern over what he perceived to be a deterioration of American Catholicism, precisely in its unwillingness to extend its post–Vatican II principles of openness and dialogue to the gay community. He did not leave, in other words, out of convenience, indifference, or lack of concern with regard to his Catholic heritage. In Albert Hirschman's terms, his exit is that of "the loyalist—that is, the member who cares—who leaves no stone unturned before he resigns himself to the painful decision to withdraw or switch."[4] I understand this man's exit to be the way he chose to exercise his role as an organic intellectual. His exit was itself an effort to assert the legitimate views of the gay community to the American hierarchy, and an exhortation to the church, as it grapples with this epidemic, to reexamine its relationship to that community.

Interacting with American Catholicism
The remaining seventeen ministers with whom I spoke chose not to exit either church or ministry. They chose rather to exercise their role as organic intellectuals by remaining, in one way or another, within the official ministry, and, in varying degrees, seeking to change the official policies and perceptions of the hierarchy. While these men and women are clearly Catholic, they are so in a different fashion than that represented in traditional teachings of the hierarchy. Generally on the progressive side, they represent what sociologist Andrew Greeley once termed "communal Catholics":

> They are loyal to the Catholic collectivity and at least sympathetic toward its heritage. At the same time, they refuse to take seriously the teaching authority of the leadership of the institutional church. Such communal Catholics are Catholic because they see nothing else in American society they want to be, out of loyalty to their past, and they are curious as to what the Catholic tradition might have that is special and unique in the contemporary world.[5]

One of the marks of such communal Catholics, Greeley predicted in 1977, would be a growing dissent from the Catholic sexual ethic.

Indeed, as Greeley has more recently noted, post–Vatican II American Catholicism has too frequently been mistakenly caricatured by the American media in terms of a "Catholicism in Crisis" paradigm that he summarizes as follows:

> The changes in the Catholic Church had created a painful crisis of conscience for American Catholics. Either they would submit to Vatican rules or leave the Church, the latter an action that would create serious problems for their superstitious Catholic souls."[6]

This distorted portrait of American Catholics, as Greeley asserts, over-looks a third alternative: Many Catholics are genuinely shaped by their interactions with other cultures within pluralistic America, yet they re-main Catholics nevertheless. They choose to remain within the church, *but do so on their own terms.*[7]

Of the eighteen men and women with whom I spoke, the seventeen who remain as ministers within the church seem to fit Greeley's portrayal of the communal Catholic. They remain official ministers, in constant interaction with their religious community and tradition, yet do so on their own terms.

A clear Catholic identity seems to manifest itself in the strong em-phasis on social justice that has shaped the way many of these ministers have come to approach the epidemic. A hospital chaplain told me how the epidemic had become an occasion in which he was able to integrate his convictions regarding social justice with his pastoral ministry:

> I had a strong interest in social justice—but I always saw it as being "out there" somewhere. In my pastoral setting, I've never had opportunity to do a lot of social justice work. So AIDS was an event, an issue of social justice, that came into my parish, the hospital.

Specifically, his convictions concerning social justice had sensitized this man to the demands of many PWAs and AIDS activists for access to adequate health care.

A similar understanding of his ministry was articulated by another minister serving as the director of an interfaith pastoral care agency. This organic intellectual described his agency's efforts as

> mining out the best of the church's tradition: being there for people when no one else is, being a voice for the voiceless. This leads us to "picket and pray," to being on the edge where the church, many churches, are afraid to go. Not the Mother Teresa approach of picking up the dying, but being an advocate of social justice. We see AIDS as a lens through which to look at the issues the church and society have never really faced: mar-ginalization of people, death, exclusion, sexuality—and we say that AIDS is not the cause of any of these, but it is the opportunity to look at them on a deeper level and to mine out of our Christian/Jewish tradition the best that we can find. I have no problem with the Mother Teresa model, but it lacks the advocacy and social justice issues, and getting at systems, and getting at the issue of poverty, the root causes for people's inability to get access to medical care. Where is the church on those is-sues? So we have structural concern, but our name is pastoral. But pasto-ral doesn't mean one-on-one care of PWAs and families, but pastorally going after these important social issues.

Yet, while maintaining a clearly Catholic identity, these ministers have done so "on their own terms." It is not just any "brand" of Catholicism with which they primarily choose to relate and identify. Although they do not embrace the same "brand" of Catholicism as Cardinal Ratzinger, for example, they nevertheless continue to see themselves as bona fide Catholics and ministers. Like their counterpart who left the church and the active ministry, these men and women cherish the developments within Catholicism since Vatican II. They value democratization and the expanded role of the laity and particularly of women in the church. They appreciate the ecumenical strides of the last twenty-five years and the increased openness of the church to the larger pluralistic American culture. They do not view responsible dissent as disloyalty.

Many of the ministers regarded their ministry as part of a grassroots movement, much like the *Comunidades de Base* of South America. They saw their collective efforts as having originated not with the bishops, but through the initiative of front-line priests, nuns, and lay people who confronted the epidemic in parishioners, neighbors, and family members. One priest, a founder of an interdenominational agency, put it this way:

> My experience of AIDS ministry is that it hasn't come from the institution, but it's come from communities of faith and it's come from the grassroots. It's come from local churches, it's come from people of faith, very frequently interdenominationally. That certainly was the history of the group I helped to establish. It was a group of people who came together out of a common concern about the spiritual needs of people with AIDS.

While maintaining a clear and strong Catholic identity, the ministers in this category also demonstrated a method of pastoral care that respects the frequently non-Catholic, and occasionally anti-Catholic, cultures and values of the parties involved. The story one priest told me comes to mind as an example. A family had arrived in town to visit their gay son who was dying of AIDS. Devoutly Catholic, they insisted— over their son's and his lover's protests—that a priest be called to administer the sacraments. When this priest arrived at the scene, he realized that it was the family that was most in need of his presence.

> I made it clear that I would not go into the son's room, and that I would respect his and his lover's space. I told the family that they were privileged guests in the lover's home and they should have respect for that.

In spending time with the family, he assured them "that their son does not need a priest and that if he has made a break with the church, it is on an institutional level and he has not made a break with God." The family got the message, and later went into their son's room to assure him that they would respect his wishes not to have a priest visit him. This priest then administered the Sacrament of the Sick—but to the family! He gave them communion, and assisted them in making funeral arrangements.

A more traditional minister might have used such a moment to reaffirm the family's perception of their son as having strayed from the true path, and might even have berated the dying son and his lover for having done so. This priest, however, an organic intellectual, provided the delicate and necessary link between the Catholic worldview of the family, their symbols and rituals, with the gay worldview of the PWA and his lover. This story of a concrete pastoral situation illustrates, I believe, the kind of cultural sensitivity that I saw repeatedly throughout my discussions with these ministers. They were able, in other words, to respect the pluralistic American context in which they were ministering.

Thus, these ministers generally seemed to me to strike a healthy balance: they remained clearly Catholic in their theology and spirituality, echoing many of the more progressive elements found in the statements of the hierarchy. Yet they did not echo the traditional sexual ethic found in the American bishops' statements. They seemed better able than the bishops to genuinely interact with others whose symbolic moral universe might be very different. They could contribute to PWAs and their loved ones from the rich arsenal of stories and rituals within their own Catholic tradition, yet do so without imposition or coercion. These ministers appeared to me to have developed a legitimate and worthwhile pastoral method in which they could both contribute to and learn from other people affected by this epidemic. While I found them to be proud of their Catholic heritage, I did not find them to be dogmatic. They were able to present a genuinely Catholic identity, but on their own terms.

Another notable characteristic of these ministers was their willingness to listen to and trust personal experience, both their own and that of others, when formulating moral judgments. Perhaps this reflects their reaction to a more conservative, and many times oppressive, Catholic worldview in which moral authority is independent of, prior to, and more powerful than an individual's own experience, a worldview in which one must submit personal intellect and experience to the will of God as expressed in the teachings of the pope and magisterium. By contrast, some of the AIDS ministers I spoke with tended to give greater weight to the experience and judgments of the individual, even to the point of reflecting at times what Robert Bellah and his colleagues have described as "expressive individualism." One minister, a woman working in a church-sponsored shelter for homeless PWAs, described her pastoral approach in these words:

> We believe that there's a spirituality within all persons, something that gives their life meaning. However I can find out what that is and provide opportunities to advance a person's spirituality. That's my goal.

Another minister, a priest/chaplain in a large, non-Catholic hospital stressed the difference between being religiously affiliated to a church and being spiritual:

> So many AIDS patients have said, "I don't experience myself as a religious person, but I do experience myself as a deeply spiritual person." The theology I operate under values narrative, the stories of people, and it assumes the presence of the sacred within people's experience. The pastoral role as I see it is to help people trust their experience, to articulate their experience, their spirituality, to affirm and celebrate that.

There is often a type of pragmatism in these ministers' approach, one that is centered around the individual's perception of his or her own emotional needs or psychological disposition. For example, a priest operating a nonprofit agency independent of the institutional church told me that he draws from whatever religious traditions or spiritualities enable an individual to be kind and to forgive. Institutional pronouncements are of less importance in his ministry.

> I appreciate Eucharist and scriptures and values of compassion. What the pope and the bishop say is to be considered, but doesn't touch my life much. I try to take what helps me be a better person. I try to forgive. I tell people, "Let's just talk about coming back to God." I try to talk about who Jesus is. I tell them, "You don't have to buy into this church stuff. What's helpful for you now at the end of your life? Who do you need to forgive?"

Other ministers, particularly those with more administrative responsibilities, explicitly repudiated any theological effort to interpret the epidemic, preferring to focus more on the practical exigencies: services to be delivered, programs to be administered, a scarcity of financial resources to be scraped together. Working long hours to keep their programs and agencies afloat, these ministers regarded theologizing about the epidemic as a luxury they could not afford. Like Susan Sontag, these ministers eschewed interpretation. They constructed the epidemic as a medical and sociopolitical problem requiring the appropriate technical treatments, strategies, and administration.

Yet in contrast to those who constructed the epidemic in either expressive individualist or administrative terms, many of the ministers I spoke with chose rather to draw from the rich tapestry of scriptural and traditional stories and images to render an explicitly Catholic construction of the epidemic. Many of them referred to the biblical stories of Jesus mingling with lepers and those who were despised by his society, and they saw these stories as metaphors for their own ministry.

I look at Jesus rubbing shoulders with people who weren't considered within the moral norms and structures of his own people. He was a far more effective teacher than if he had stayed in the temple precincts. He was in the streets, with all kinds of people who hadn't heard the message.

One minister drew metaphors from the stories of Exodus and Exile in the Hebrew Scriptures, stories of a people formed and strengthened through their common journey and struggle, to describe the effect of the epidemic on individuals and the gay community as a whole.

For me this experience reinforces the lessons of Exodus and Exile. There's a forging of character and a purifying of intent that takes place when a people experience adversity in its most extreme. By necessity, despite the impingement on our resources, there is a reflectivity that occurs. The people I've come to know up to the time of their death have taught me what is really important. . . . If the reign of God is something we're still moving toward, then God is still working with us toward the transformation of individual lives and communities.

Another minister, a Franciscan priest, drew metaphors from his own Franciscan heritage to construct the PWA as a privileged place of contact with God. He found within the story of St. Francis a challenge to grow spiritually in his own ministry as did Francis in his.

In my perspective as a Franciscan, those that have HIV infection are a gift to us, a place where we can receive God. As Francis knew, he had to let go of all the goodies in his life that had nothing to do with the gospel, and to reach out to those that were afflicted and to find in them the face of Christ and his spiritual nourishment.

In short, these latter ministers seemed to draw explicitly from the reservoir of stories, images, and symbols found within the larger Catholic culture when interpreting their own and their clients' experiences of sickness and death. This facility in referring to the stories of the tradition seemed to allow them to link their individual lives and stories, the tragedies of their own lives and of the people to whom they ministered, with a larger community, a larger story, a larger universe of meaning. Such an ability not only enabled them to live and work more gracefully within the epidemic, but also to overcome the cold isolation that can accompany associating oneself with a stigmatized disease. Their Catholic identity, its treasury of stories and traditions, served them well.

As organic intellectuals, these ministers were able to link alienated gay PWAs with their Catholic heritage. One minister stated that, in doing this, he often found it necessary to ask his clients for forgiveness for the ways in which the teachings and practices of the institutional church had hurt them.

> Very frequently the experience is one of alienation and disintegration. As a pastor and religious person, I think I can help people do some reconciling and gain some integration. From the reconciling aspect, as a religious person I ask forgiveness for the way the church has abandoned them, or only been a judge. This is the integration part of what I do. . . . Wherever it feels useful, I try to help them integrate their experience of church, to reconnect some of the religious symbols of their past. If their symbols are found in traditional religious expression, I try to help them reclaim that.

The difficulties these ministers expressed most frequently had to do with the context of the American church today, a context in which the Vatican—with its strong aversion to gay sexual expression, gay rights, and the use of condoms—has decisively shaped the American hierarchy's construction of the epidemic. Concretely, this has meant that each of these ministers has had to find a way to manage the conflict between personal convictions about such issues as homosexuality and the need for safer sex education on the one hand, and, on the other hand, their charge to publicly represent (or at least not publicly oppose) the official teachings of the hierarchy to whom they owe their obedience, and sometimes their livelihood. In this context, each seemed to position himself or herself in one of two different ways: (1) maintaining an official position in a parish, chancery office, or Catholic social agency, and in that role remaining publicly silent on the issues of homosexuality and safer sex, while privately affirming the gay identity of clients and encouraging their use of safer sex; (2) moving to the margins of the institutional structure of the church where one has less direct command over church resources and policies, yet where one can speak one's moral convictions forthrightly in both the public and private forums.

Maintaining a Mainline Position

This first group includes men and women in such professional, salaried roles as director of AIDS services for Catholic Charities, director of AIDS services within an archdiocese or a parish, and a priest doing pastoral work in a parish. In each instance, the minister, while serving the needs of a diversity of people, is located more centrally in the Catholic world. He or she relates to the institutional church from within, while also seeking to relate credibly to the gay community.

In working within such positions, these ministers are characterized by a split between their public and private positions on the more controversial issues within the epidemic such as safer sex. The director of a Catholic Charities AIDS agency comes to mind here.

He spoke to me with pride in what his agency had accomplished through its shelter for homeless PWAs, its counseling programs and emergency funds. He noted that, in a time of tremendous shortage of money and of burnout of people within the gay community, the church's resources become all the more necessary in battling the epidemic. At the same time, as an openly gay man himself, he could relish the irony that he and so many other openly gay and lesbian people were, with the archbishop's full knowledge, on the payroll of this Catholic agency. Yet this man, proud of both his agency and of his gay identity, found that working in such a job carried its share of problems.

He told me of the time he was asked by the media to render an opinion about the archbishop's public opposition to a local ballot initiative that would grant medical benefits to the partners of gay/lesbian employees of the city. This man's statement to the media, while being deliberately ambiguous (he was quoted as saying simply that the archbishop's position was "amazing"), had nevertheless prompted a reprimanding phone call from the archbishop. As a result of such an experience, he had decided to tone down his own political voice on such controversial issues as gay rights and condom distribution for the sake of developing and maintaining a viable AIDS service program under Catholic auspices. "Gay political issues have nothing to do with AIDS," he told me, "so we don't address them in the media."

Another minister, this one working out of a Catholic parish in which he is directly answerable to the pastor, told me that, in private, he and other AIDS ministers were very forthright in advocating the use of condoms and safer sex to the people they were serving. On a public level, however, they refused to address the issue, content to do what they were able to do within the given ecclesiastical constraints:

Our concern is with people already ill and needing practical assistance. Public health people are in a better place, and have more liberty, to talk safer sex than we do. We do what we can do within our constraints as part of the church. We leave the other issues alone. Other people are addressing them well, and meanwhile we can do other worthwhile things.

Yet another minister, the head nurse on the AIDS unit of a large urban Catholic hospital, spoke of trying to balance the policies of the hospital with his obligations as a health professional and his own convictions about human sexuality. He mentioned, for example, having to hide from view of hospital administrators the issues of the local gay newspaper delivered to the floor each Wednesday. He further mentioned that when the hospital was seeking support volunteers for patients in the AIDS ward, he was forbidden by hospital administrators to place an advertisement in the gay newspaper.

With regard to his professional obligations to provide adequate information concerning HIV transmission and prevention, this minister stated that he generally chose his words very carefully, depending on his audience at the time:

It depends on who I'm talking to. When I go to _____ University or St. _____ College and talk to nursing students, I talk about our professional responsibility. Even if we are in a Catholic institution, we need to exercise some judgment and some prudence. I will not put up posters on the unit advocating condom use. If I'm sitting with a patient and they are asking questions about safe sex, I have the responsibility as a health care professional to give people the information they need to make informed choices. I can say that though this is not what the institution believes, it is medically proven that if you are not going to abstain then you need to do some things to take care of yourself and you need to make some choices. I'm sure I'm bending the rule.... So I try to be sensitive to what the church teaches, I try to be sensitive to the sisters who run the hospital. I'm not here to make life uncomfortable for myself or for anybody else. At the same time, there is a responsibility I have as a health care professional to provide the information. The choice the person I'm counseling makes is up to them.

Walking the line between two cultures in conflict has meant, even beyond a professional ambivalence, an internal conflict and wrestling for some of the ministers I interviewed. One of them, a priest assisting in a parish with strong AIDS outreach services, told me of a remark made to him by a parishioner, a lesbian with AIDS who had been participating in a support group he facilitated within the parish. She told him how strange it seemed to her that she would be coming to a Catholic church for assistance. He paraphrased her: "It's like being Jewish during the Holocaust and coming to the good Nazis and asking for help." This minister told me that his recognition of the church's oppression of gays and lesbians made him feel "guilt and shame" to be a Catholic priest during this epidemic. He described himself as "both the oppressed and the oppressor at the same time." He drew an analogy from the Twelve Step movement to describe the ecclesiastical situation in which he ministered, referring to the church as a "dysfunctional family." For all of its dysfunctionality, it achieves much that is positive, and even as you recognize its destructive aspects and go about trying to correct them, you still remain loyal to the family.

I'm an adult child of an alcoholic family system, so I know how to be a member of a dysfunctional family, even though I don't necessarily agree with all that's going on in the family. The church as a dysfunctional family makes a lot of sense to me. So apart from the guilt and the shame, it's like this is reality. And the support group is being offered. And where we're at with that woman who spoke about coming to the good Nazis is that she expresses a lot of gratitude that we are there.

Another minister who formally represents her archbishop on various AIDS agency boards and task forces throughout the city mentioned her interior struggle in being expected to represent a position that is at odds with what she knows as a community health nurse and with her own moral convictions regarding sexuality. Given the discrepancy between what the hierarchy teaches and what people have come to know from their own experience,

people go ahead and make up their own mind. I'm old enough, and I make my own personal decisions, so I'm comfortable with that. But when I'm speaking as a representative of the archdiocese, then I feel that my role limits me in what I can say. That's a real area of conflict for me. Sometimes I feel like I'm not really being true to what I believe. I need to adequately represent the archdiocese. All employees here have to sign a statement that they won't talk about condoms or birth control when working with clients. Fortunately I didn't have to sign that statement, but it's in my contract with the Catholic university where I teach. That puts pressures on me. I know what people want me to say, yet what I feel I *can* say are two different things.

The situation these ministers described—of being required to say one thing in public while believing something very different in private, of being both an oppressor and oppressed—brings to mind the reflections of Václav Havel, the president of the former Czechoslovakia, about the hitherto double life of Eastern Europeans. The totalitarian state demanded signs of outward conformity. All you had to do was keep quiet, or, when forced to speak, use the right words. It was a matter of systematically saying one thing in public and another in private. Havel described the situation in Eastern Europe as a "contaminated moral environment." In his New Year's Day address he said, "All of us have become accustomed to the totalitarian system, accepted it as an unalterable fact and, therefore, kept it running. . . . None of us is merely a victim of it, because all of us helped create it together." The crucial line of conflict, he said, ran not between the people and the state but rather through the middle of each person, "for everyone in his or her own way is both a victim and supporter of the system."

Like the people of Eastern Europe as characterized by Václav Havel, these ministers in the more mainline positions are both supporters and victims of the ecclesiastical system. As supporters of that system, they are able to utilize the institution's resources of money and people and buildings in delivering much-needed services to people suffering from AIDS. They can legitimately assert with pride what their church has accomplished in this regard. At the same time, as victims of the ecclesiastical system, they often suffer the effects of "cognitive dissonance" and the psychic split between their personal convictions and their public roles.

Indeed, by remaining in their mainstream positions, these ministers no doubt exercise an important influence on the church by informing appropriate church authorities of the practical needs of PWAs for social services. But are they effective in the larger cultural matter of representing to church authorities the legitimate features of gay sexuality and the desires and aspirations of gay people for acceptance in American culture? Are they effective when it comes to changing the American hierarchy's proscription of condoms and safer sex education? In these latter respects, they are clearly less effective. The professional positions of these ministers require them to maintain a cautious—one could say deadly—silence with regard to these critical issues. In this respect, their ability to play a credible role within the gay community and the larger American discourse on AIDS is often severely curtailed.

Part of the reason for this lack of effectiveness has to do with the current intransigence of the hierarchy and the unlikelihood of any official change in the Catholic sexual ethic for many years. But the ineffectiveness of these ministers in this regard also stems precisely from the way in which they have positioned themselves within the institution. Their paychecks as well as their professional credibility derive from the institution itself. The price of seeking to influence the hierarchy by exiting their positions, or of explicitly challenging the hierarchy's position, is therefore formidable. Significant voice to change church teachings with regard to homosexuality and safer sex is therefore less likely to come from these mainline ministers.

Moving to the Margins

The reverse is the case for those who find a position at the margins of that structure. While able to exert less influence over the allocation of church resources in delivering social services, these ministers are freer to speak forthrightly to the hierarchy and the larger American culture concerning the need for a more enlightened sexual ethic and the practical need for safer sex education in combating the spread of AIDS. Given the conflict between the institutional church and the gay community, these ministers, while maintaining their official status as ministers, have opted to pull away from the centers of church authority.

Thus, the ministers in this category work primarily in situations that are not affiliated with the institutional church. They include a priest who is the head of AIDS pastoral care for a large, urban, non-Catholic hospital; a layman who ministers on behalf of Dignity, the ostracized organization of gay and lesbian Catholics; a laywoman in a financially independent shelter for homeless PWAs; a priest who established and administers an independent, financially struggling nonprofit program for caregivers of PWAs; another priest who directs an interfaith pastoral care network; a nun who works with disadvantaged youth in an ecumenical ministry program.

One priest, reflecting on the history of the interdenominational agency he was influential in establishing, described the balance he and his agency had hoped to achieve:

> We felt our effectiveness required that we have one foot clearly in ecclesial communities, and one foot in the gay community, but not fully identified with either. I think we've established credibility in both communities, and, more recently, in the Hispanic community. Frankly, I've seen the interdenominational support as guilt money: "You go do what you're doing, and we'll support you, because we can't do it." Our independence from the institution actually enables us to do things we could not otherwise do—without getting caught up in teachings on sexuality and condoms. They [i.e., denominational leaders] don't have responsibility for what we do, and unless someone is a witch-hunter, they're not

going to get caught into that. In terms of our effectiveness, we've never had to be political.

How did these ministers come to find themselves at the margins of the institution? One priest's story seemed particularly dramatic. This priest came out as a gay man while working in a parish. The journey had led him to take a leave of absence from official ministry for a time, but had not diminished his desire to be a priest. Eventually, he approached the local archbishop and requested restoration of his faculties to administer the sacraments and to preach. The archbishop granted the request, but would not allow him to become incardinated into the archdiocese or provide him with medical, dental, and retirement benefits. The relationship that has ensued has been distant yet cordial, allowing him to validly minister as an ordained priest, yet consigning him to the margins of the institution.

> I wanted gay people to know that God loves them. I really wanted to bring Eucharist to people. I love celebrating Eucharist. I wanted to be a priest, but not in the official structure. I correspond with the archbishop. He knows I'm doing good work, and the agency I run has a good reputation in the community.

These men and women are, for practical purposes, financially independent of the institutional church and not dependent on the local bishop for their livelihood. While this gives them a certain freedom, it also means that, unlike their mainline counterparts, they have fewer institutional and financial resources at their disposal. The priest I just mentioned runs a nonprofit agency providing services to caregivers of PWAs. He started the agency with a twenty-dollar donation from a friend, and has continued to support the effort entirely through private contributions. "Raising money is very hard these days," he told me, and "I have to have a constant trust that God will provide." Yet he also told me of the resentment he sometimes feels when, for example, he sees a three-million-dollar church under construction in the suburbs, while he is told by church officials that they have no money to help him pay the rent.

Yet despite the financial struggles, the position of relative independence enjoyed by these ministers has allowed them a greater freedom than their mainline counterparts in speaking about such things as condoms and safer sex. As they do this, they are able to avoid the political maneuvering and doublespeak occasionally required of those working in parishes and chancery offices.

114   The Challenges of Catholic AIDS Ministry

One of these ministers, a priest working in a non-Catholic hospital, told me that he had once stated in the public media that he considered the official teaching on condoms to be "immoral." One nun who works for an interdenominational street ministry openly provides safer sex information to groups and individuals at community shelters. "What I'm doing, the chancery office would not want to know about," she told me. Yet another minister described the common sense approach he uses when speaking to lay audiences at local congregations, both Catholic and Protestant.

We're able to talk about safe sex and condoms. I've always said that condoms for our church are a real problem, but will you deny your children and grandchildren that piece of information, a piece that might save their lives? Sure, you want them to follow the church's teachings just as you don't want them to drink and drive. But what do you tell your children about drinking and driving? Don't do it, but if you do it, call me and I'll come get you. And people respond to that. So it's not going to a congregation and throwing out condoms, but trying to help them understand. . . . We've been able to do that kind of serious education.

Yet while establishing an independent base, these organic intellectuals have preserved definite links with the institutional church. In fact, in one archdiocese, ministers in this particular category were appointed by the archbishop to serve on his AIDS advisory task force and played an influential role in shaping his pastoral letter on HIV. Moreover, while it is true that, from a canonical standpoint, all of these ministers could conceivably be disciplined for not taking a more orthodox approach to the epidemic, in reality none of them feared such an outcome. In fact, several of these ministers mentioned that they felt the local ordinary was secretly supportive of them and their efforts. "If you cornered the archbishop," one of these ministers told me, "he would approve of our efforts. From a political standpoint, he can support us, yet speak of us as an independent group that does not represent the archdiocese should the right wing object."

Since they do not depend upon the institution for either their livelihood or their professional standing, they have a greater freedom to influence the discourse on AIDS, both within the church and in the larger American society. They are able to publicly dissent from the hierarchy's position.

The AIDS Metaphors of Pastoral Caregivers

In the previous chapter, I described the construction of AIDS as enunciated by the American Catholic bishops. In this chapter, I have described another group of actors within the American Catholic discourse on AIDS. In many respects, the construction of AIDS by the men and women in this chapter is similar to that of the bishops: for example, it draws upon the American Catholic social justice tradition, insists on standing in solidarity with those suffering from the disease, and, in several cases, interprets the experiences of people with AIDS according to the metaphors found within the scriptures and traditional stories and symbols of Catholicism, thereby giving those experiences a uniquely redemptive meaning. In these respects it can be said that the pastoral ministers in this chapter reaffirm the more progressive elements found in the bishops' letters.

At the same time, the construction of AIDS by these ministers differs in significant ways from that of the bishops. These ministers, if not fully self-identified as gay themselves, are very empathetic toward the gay community, recognizing the legitimacy of its sexual expressions, its hopes and aspirations for acceptance and liberation. Moreover, they are in constant interaction with gay people suffering from this disease, and have thereby witnessed the nobility and grace to be found among members of the gay community in these tragic times. Consequently, their construction of AIDS, unlike that of the bishops, evolves out of and reflects their own positive interaction with the gay community. They do not understand homosexuality as a violation of the natural law as do the bishops. Nor do they understand AIDS as the logical result of violating the traditional sexual ethic. When ministering to gay men, they do not try to ignore the latters' gay identity and network of relationships. Nor do they insist, as do the bishops, that the use of condoms would merely condone and encourage behavior that is immoral. Thus, they stand apart from the bishops in some key areas.

There were some differences among these ministers themselves, primarily in the ways they positioned themselves vis-à-vis the institutional church. One minister left the official ministry and the church in order to more freely embrace a gay religious sensibility. Some ministers chose to work in mainline positions within the institution. These were able to command significant financial and popular resources in service of PWAs, but had to wrestle with professional and personal doublespeak as a result of their position within a "totalitarian system." Still other ministers chose to work in more marginal positions. While these were not able to command the significant resources of the church as they went about their ministry, they were able to speak honestly and publicly about what they regarded as the practical needs of the epidemic and of those most affected by it.

I stated at the beginning of this chapter that the final Catholic construction of AIDS would depend on whether a more traditional or a more progressive worldview became successful in establishing a clear cultural hegemony. I also mentioned that, since the American bishops, in some important respects, have operated from a more traditional worldview in constructing this disease, a change in the hierarchy's position would occur only if the more progressive voices were to be heard more clearly by the bishops. Critical to the dynamic is the role of the organic intellectuals described in this chapter.

The more important issues within the epidemic are cultural, having to do with the moral evaluation of sexual expressions. In the long run, the energies of this country cannot be effectively marshalled against this disease unless there is a cultural shift that will allow us as a nation to take the steps that are needed. Such steps, as the surgeon general and other public health officials have asserted, include the encouragement of safer sex.

When it comes to speaking to these larger cultural issues involved in this epidemic, the ministers in the more marginal roles seem to have the greater potential effectiveness. Maintaining a critical distance both from the gay community and from the church, yet with ties to each, they are able to exercise an invaluable mediating role. They are able to carry the Catholic concerns for compassion and social justice as well as the rich Catholic repertoire of symbols and stories into the larger cultural discourse taking place within this country. At the same time, since they are free to speak forthrightly about such issues as sexual morality and safer sex education, they are able to responsibly challenge the traditional Catholic sexual ethic and the unconscionable danger in which it currently places the lives of many people.

The American Catholic church currently lacks a credible moral voice within the larger cultural discourse on AIDS. Clearly, some new voices need to be heard within the church if this situation is to change. The organic intellectuals described in this chapter represent some of the voices urging a change in the bishops' official construction of AIDS. Their success in being heard both by average Catholics as well as by the bishops—their success, in other words, in forging a cultural hegemony on this issue—will determine in part whether the American Catholic church will be able to assume a position of credible moral leadership within the American discourse on AIDS.

5 The Gay Community and the Catholic Church: Battleground or Common Ground?

AIDS is a moment when the Catholic church and the gay community share a common desire to alleviate human suffering. This convergence of two conflicting cultures can be either mutually enriching or mutually destructive. It can either hasten the end of the epidemic, or prolong it unnecessarily.

As one who prizes both the gay and the Catholic cultures, I celebrate those instances when these two communities enrich each other, as when, for example, an elderly and conservative Southern archbishop reads the names of persons who died of AIDS at a display of the NAMES Project Quilt, or when a Catholic parish welcomes gay men and lesbians and develops programs that respect their unique values and needs. And I also lament those other moments—far too many than are necessary, it seems—when these two cultures shore up their moral boundaries and excommunicate each other, whether in condemnatory statements from the Vatican or in the stereotypes of Catholics promoted by many AIDS activists and members of the gay press. It was out of lamentation over what has gone wrong in the interactions between the gay and Catholic cultures in this time of AIDS—and a desire to overcome it—that I chose to write about this topic.

The demonstration outside New York's St. Patrick's Cathedral, as I noted in the Introduction, highlighted the fact that the American hierarchy's construction of AIDS has been very problematic for many of the people most concerned about the effects of the epidemic. Indeed, the meaning ascribed to AIDS by the bishops has left even national leaders charged with public education and health care perplexed and outraged.

That the Catholic construction of AIDS came to be so forcefully rejected is, for some Catholics like Cardinal O'Connor, a great irony. The church, after all, has provided a vast array of services to people with AIDS from the very beginning of the epidemic. Cardinal O'Connor himself has been a member of the National Commission on AIDS. How, such church members ask, could anyone find fault with the Catholic response to AIDS?

The answer is that although the hierarchy undeniably has made a generous contribution to the well-being of many PWAs through its many social services and programs, it nevertheless has constructed AIDS in a way that is insulting and jarring to many contemporary Americans, particularly gay men and lesbians. While providing many needed services, it has also regarded the epidemic as a moment in which to reaffirm the traditional sexual ethic, thereby effectively shoring up its own moral boundaries against those most affected by the disease. In this view, AIDS, though not a punishment from God as some Protestant fundamentalists have asserted, is nevertheless a result of violating the sexual code. With this construction of AIDS, the hierarchy has extended compassion with one hand and harsh judgment and condemnation with the other. This mixed message has weakened the credibility of the Catholic response to the epidemic, at least in the minds of many at the forefront of the war against AIDS. Such a construction of AIDS is an affront to those gay men and lesbians who have just begun, after many years of struggle, to own and enjoy the unique sexual heritage that is theirs. Such a construction, moreover, fails to take seriously the larger reconstruction of sexuality that has taken place in the West, especially since Freud.

Of course, the American Catholic hierarchy is not the only group on the American cultural landscape to have constructed AIDS in this way. Indeed, the battle to define the meaning of AIDS is part of a larger cultural war currently being waged in this country, as James Davison Hunter and others have recently observed. The divisions within American culture are no longer drawn along denominational lines. Rather, they are drawn between adherents of an orthodox worldview (which, for example, opposes the Equal Rights Amendment, abortion rights, gay rights, and various forms of contemporary artistic expression as found in the work of a Robert Mapplethorpe) and those of a progressive one. These cultural divisions are to be found within each religious denomination today, as well as among those who regard themselves as secularists or atheists.

The Catholic church, like most other denominations and communities in this country, has within its ranks both orthodox and progressive members. When it comes to defining the meaning of AIDS, the hierarchy has aligned itself, in some critical respects, with the more orthodox factions in that cultural war, defining AIDS as the result of violating the sexual code. Their orthodox position is mitigated, however, by the fact that many priests and laity, including those I discussed in chapter 4, find themselves on the other side of that war, defining AIDS as a disease rather than as a result of moral failure, a natural tragedy like an earthquake or a hurricane in the face of which we must reaffirm life and culture, including gay culture, all the more vigorously. Which side will succeed in establishing a cultural hegemony in the larger American landscape, and which side will carry the greater weight in defining the meaning of AIDS, is not yet clear. It is clear, however, that the outcome of this larger cultural war will significantly shape what comes to be the specifically Catholic construction of both homosexuality and AIDS.

Pending the outcome of the larger cultural war in the United States, no real consensus on the meaning of AIDS will be able to emerge unless both the gay community and the church tone down their mutual denunciations and excommunications. Without a sincere effort to locate a common ground, we are left with only the continuation of the current warfare.

Thus, while the American hierarchy has at times desecrated what the gay community has come to regard as sacred, namely, their relationships and forms of sexual expression, the gay community has also occasionally desecrated what Catholics regard as sacred as, for example, in the demonstration at St. Patrick's, with its disruption of the liturgy and, in one especially unfortunate moment, the desecration of a consecrated wafer. Far from being similar to the tactics employed by Martin Luther King, which sought to locate common ground and to bring previously hostile factions into dialogue, these actions, both by the Vatican and by some gay leaders, have only contributed to the unfortunate impasse. They have only intensified the bitter conflict at a time when energies should be directed at defeating the common enemy, AIDS.

It is ironic that the gay community, which so highly values the right to free expression, should react so vigorously when the Catholic hierarchy seeks to exercise that very right by stating its own moral position. It is even more ironic, however, that the American Catholic church should contribute to such an impasse. In an earlier era, Catholics themselves suffered from ostracism and exclusion from the larger American discourse. That has changed and today, especially since the election of John F. Kennedy to the presidency and the socioeconomic advances made by American Catholics, the American Catholic church is seen as a respected partner within that discourse. This makes it doubly ironic that the hierarchy of that same church should now seek to ostracize and exclude the gay community from participation in that larger discourse. Indeed, what John Courtney Murray once described as the warlike relationship between Catholics and Protestants now seems to characterize the relationship between the Catholic hierarchy and the gay community:

> We are not really a group of men singly engaged in the search for truth, relying solely on the means of persuasion, entering into dignified communication with each other, content politely to correct opinions with which we do not agree. As a matter of fact, the variant ideas and allegiances among us are entrenched as social powers; they occupy ground; they have developed interests; and they possess the means to fight for them. The real issues of truth that arise are complicated by secondary issues of power and prestige, which not seldom become primary.[1]

The repeated showdowns between local bishops and AIDS activists are a contemporary manifestation of the "structure of war," the term with which Murray once characterized Catholic-Protestant relations in an earlier era.

What needs to occur now is a ceasefire and a commitment to a larger American universe capable of holding all of us together, even with all of our differences. Recall here the expansive and inclusive universe of Gandhi that I mentioned in chapter 3, a universe that could honor and hold together both Hindu and Muslim. Within such a larger universe, true discourse can occur because there is found in that universe "a core of agreement, accord, concurrence, acquiescence. We hold certain truths; therefore we can argue about them."[2] Indeed, as the bishops stated so well in their first statement on AIDS, but somehow lost in their second statement: "We believe that there are certain basic values present in our society which transcend religious or sectarian boundaries and which can constitute a common basis for these social efforts."[3]

What is required by these two warring factions for such a discourse to become possible? On the Catholic side, there first of all needs to be a loosening of the tradition regarding sexual ethics. The matter of Catholic sexual ethics can no longer be viewed as a closed case, as though it were a divinely revealed and absolutely unchangeable truth. The socially constructed nature of the traditional Catholic sexual ethic as derived from Greco-Roman Stoicism must now be acknowledged. In that understanding—which the Church came to regard as ontologically true and an element of natural law, not simply a human construct—nonprocreative sexual expression is contrary to nature, and hence homosexual sexual expression and the use of such contraceptives as condoms are proscribed. Other sexual metaphors derived from other Judeo-Christian sources (e.g., the Song of Songs, the Yahwist creation account, the traditional Catholic principle that grace builds on nature) remain ignored.

The American Catholic hierarchy has clung to its traditional constructions of sexuality despite the fact that the larger constructions of sexuality in the West have changed dramatically within the past century, particularly since Freud. The hierarchy has likewise been unwilling to acknowledge more recent shifts in American sexuality brought on by the women's movements, the sexual revolution, and the emergence of a bona fide gay culture and community. The Catholic hierarchy has remained impervious to all of these larger cultural shifts and developments, unwilling to dialogue, rigidly clinging to a sexual norm that makes less and less sense to more and more Catholics.

The fact that the American hierarchy has remained so aloof from such significant cultural currents is a direct result of the reassertion by the papal curia of the traditional authority structure of the Catholic church. Within traditional Roman Catholicism, church authority plays the primary role in establishing and validating one's individual identity. One goes to an ordained church authority, for example, in order to be absolved of sin and receive assurance of being in good standing with God. The other sacraments, the channels of divine grace, are likewise administered by church authorities.

This traditional Catholic context represents what Richard Merleman has called a "tight-bounded" moral community in which moral obligation tends to be rigid and fixed, viewed by its members as a "given" of social life. Such a communal structure tends to create a mindset in which an individual looks for salvation not in his or her own interior life, but in the authority structure of the church. It is the opposite of "loose-bounded" moral communities in which the individual, not the social group, becomes the final arbiter of moral judgment.[4]

In the current AIDS discourse in the United States, we find the bishops on one side, following the lead of the Vatican, reasserting a traditional "tight-bounded" moral authority structure. On the other side are those voices in the post-Enlightenment cultural landscape that place primacy on individual experience and responsibility, freedom from repressive boundaries, destruction of traditional roles, and rejection of oppressively communitarian ideals and practices. These latter voices include the cultural currents of expressive individualism and liberal privatism of the 1960s and 1970s, from which the gay/lesbian movement as we now know it has emerged.

What is currently needed is not the weakening of Catholic community or identity, nor the abdication of a "tight-bounded" Catholic identity in favor of a "loose-bounded" one. Rather, Catholicism's moral boundaries need to be reexamined and redefined. The traditional definition of a "good Catholic" now so vigorously asserted by the papal curia needs to be transformed, broadened, and rendered more inclusive.

Second, as so many of the ministers I described in chapter 4 said repeatedly, the Catholic hierarchy must be willing to seriously listen to the gay community. Gay men and lesbians have gained a considerable amount of wisdom over the years of this epidemic—wisdom about sexuality and relationships, as well as about suffering and death. What does the hierarchy stand to lose by listening to these experiences and reflections? As feminist theologian Mary Hunt asserts:

> We do not need to judge gay men by calling their activities depraved. Nor do we want gay men calling us prudish. Only after we know a lot about each other do we dare to evaluate. For now, we need everyone in the community to pull together, since AIDS will not await our musings.[5]

Moreover, as former Seattle Archbishop Raymond Hunthausen once asserted before he was censured by the Vatican, "we will never discover the right answers unless we are willing to go into dialogue with those who are struggling with the issue [of gay/lesbian sexuality] in terms of their Catholic faith."[6]

It is certainly likely that the American bishops, had they been freer from Vatican pressure, would have taken a more benign position regarding gays and AIDS.[7] Perhaps more dialogue would have taken place. Largely because of Vatican influence, the American bishops have refused to dialogue openly with the gay community, fearing that to do so would legitimize what the Vatican and many conservative bishops regard as sinful behavior. The American hierarchy, consequently, has not benefited from the collective wisdom (and street savvy) that has emerged within the gay community throughout the course of this epidemic. Lacking the wisdom it could have received through dialogue with the gay community, the bishops' construction of AIDS has come to be markedly different from those generated by sectors of American society that have seriously engaged in such dialogue—for example, American medicine, social services, and government.

The hierarchy is unquestionably capable of listening to people of different worldviews, values, and symbols, and this is evident in the consultative processes they used when drafting their pastoral letters on war and peace and on the economy. Listening to other cultures has also been evident in their participation in the ecumenical movement. The fact that the bishops have so willingly listened to military officials, Wall Street magnates, and leaders of other religious denominations makes it all the more puzzling that they should have neglected to listen to leaders of the gay community when they drafted their two statements on AIDS. A conversion among the bishops is needed here. As Robert Bellah and colleagues have written concerning religious denominations in America:

> America's major denominations can no longer escape or insulate themselves by schism or segmentation from those who live and believe differently. They can no longer withdraw from public affairs in return for the state's mere tolerance. They are now enabled, and compelled, to sustain conciliar dialogue without schism, and to draw critically on related religious movements for their own reform. Now more than ever the churches can, and must, engage the larger public and the state in moral argument and education.[8]

Third, in order for a viable discourse between the hierarchy and the gay community to occur, the "contaminated moral environment" within the Catholic church itself needs to be addressed. Indeed, the bishops of the world have already acknowledged that "anyone who ventures to speak to people about justice must first be just in their eyes."[9]

Given the current power arrangements within the Catholic world, church leaders dare not speak their convictions in an open forum for fear of reprisals from higher-ups. Doublespeak reigns. Groups of loyal gay Catholics such as members of Dignity and New Ways Ministry are barred from church premises. Dedicated gay clergy are forced to remain in the closet. In such an environment, it is not easy to sustain an honest discussion about sexual ethics. Communication, to use Jurgen Habermas's phrase, is thus systematically distorted. Before the hierarchy can credibly enter the larger American discourse on AIDS, this scandal internal to the church must be addressed.

This means that the pluriformity of Catholicism needs to be consciously reappropriated. Just as there needs to be a reaffirmation of a larger universe within American society that can hold both Catholics and gays in dialogue, so there also needs to be a broader definition of "Catholic" that can include a greater diversity of people. As two American Catholic theologians have asserted:

> By honoring a plurality of myths, rituals, and institutions in the church, we confess to the splendid freedom of God expressed in wonderful multiplicity. A theological problem with present Vatican control over the whole church is the identification of God's will with the will of John Paul II or of Cardinal Ratzinger. The freedom of God and the gifts of the Spirit would be more truly respected in a decentralized and pluralistic church.[10]

These writers go on to say that "[a] democratic church would find a balanced way of incorporating gays and lesbians into its structures."[11]

A more consciously pluriform Catholicism need not mean a weakening of Catholic community or identity. Indeed, central to Catholic self-understanding is the beautiful Pauline symbol of the church as the "body of Christ," in which all the members are organically related to the others, "individually members of one another" (Romans 12:5), yet also diverse. In Corinth, where the community experienced a genuine problem of disunity and fragmentation, Paul reminded them that "we who are many are one body" (1 Corinthians 10:17). He encouraged them to acknowledge and celebrate their diversity as individuals: "If all the members were alike, where would the body be?" (1 Corinthians 12:19) And yet, he continued, although "there are, indeed, many members, there is but one body," in which all the members are organically joined to each other such that "if one member suffers, all the members suffer with it; if one member is honored, all the members share its joy" (1 Corinthians 12:20, 26).[12] The unifying element is "the same Spirit who produces all these gifts, distributing them to each as he wills" (1 Corinthians 12:11).

Thus, although individuals differ and pluriformity exists, there is no need for fragmentation and schism to follow. There is all the more reason for the members to stay together, for each requires the complement of the other. "The eye cannot say to the hand, 'I do not need you,' any more than the head can say to the feet, 'I do not need you'" (1 Corinthians 12:21). Thus, the Pauline text gives an image of a genuine catholicity that does not seek uniformity in the life of the church, but rather a unity in diversity.[13] It is within such a community, not apart from it, that an individual, with all of her or his uniqueness, can come to flourish with dignity. The retrieval of this Pauline understanding of the church is critical today as the American church wrestles with the cultural definition of AIDS.

Because the church remains one in its diversity, it is possible for discussions and vigorous debates to occur as to the meaning of AIDS and of homosexuality. As the great theologian Karl Rahner once stated:

We must become accustomed to such dissonances within the Church. We must learn to understand that tensions do not have to destroy the unity of confession, the will to obedience and love. Both sides must become accustomed to this: the official leadership, which must not think that in the Church calm or silence is the first and last "civic duty"; the laity, who must not think that, because of the fundamental possibility of theological differences of opinion and because of the possibility of withholding obedience in a particular case, an arbitrary stance in theological matters and a fundamental revolutionary hostility toward the official leadership are the ideal attitudes.[14]

The sacred canopy of Catholicism is durable enough to remain intact, even as it shelters a wider diversity than the current Vatican administration is willing to acknowledge.

Fourth, those within the church that can play the most pivotal role in a Catholic reconstruction of AIDS are such groups as Dignity and New Ways Ministry, as well as the ministers I mentioned in the last chapter who are positioned at the margins of the church. With one foot in the gay community and one foot in the church, yet independent of both, these organic intellectuals are able to provide the necessary links and translations between these two conflicting cultures, and yet do so without fear of reprisals should they also speak words of challenge to either side. Very frequently, they not only have ties to the local bishop, but also to Catholic laity in parishes who volunteer time and money to assist PWAs. Strengthening their voice could help develop a new "cultural hegemony," reshaping the Catholic discourse on AIDS along lines more sensitive to the lived experiences of gay PWAs.

In order for them to be effective within the church, it will be necessary for these ministers to remain fluent in their use of Catholic language, articulating the experience of AIDS in terms of the traditional stories, symbols, metaphors, and theology of Catholicism. The languages of expressive individualism or of administrative cost-benefit analysis, for example, are not only inadequate in describing the many dimensions of people's experiences; they also are less effective when speaking within a Catholic context. Mother Teresa's description of a person with AIDS as "Jesus in a distressing disguise" is likely to be far more powerful and meaningful to a Catholic audience—and to many others as well.

Moreover, these organic intellectuals could strengthen their presence through active mobilization within the church. Through such organizations as the National Catholic AIDS Network (NCAN), these ministers could "lobby" the hierarchy, introducing new data into the hierarchy's discussions, raising critical reflections about the course of the Catholic response to AIDS. Such an organization could, moreover, join forces with other groups within the church who have common interests in bringing about change—such groups as CORPUS and the Women's Ordination Conference.

To summarize, the inadequate construction of AIDS by the American hierarchy is symptomatic of the contaminated moral environment found within American Catholicism today. Had the power structure of American Catholicism not been so heavily dominated by Vatican interests, and had that structure allowed an honest discourse on sexuality to take place, the American Catholic hierarchy's construction of AIDS might have looked very different from what has thus far emerged. It is now necessary to recognize the socially constructed nature of the traditional Catholic sexual ethic and the power structure that maintains it. It is time, through genuine dialogue with the gay community and others, for the American hierarchy to begin the formulation of a new construction, both of sexuality and of AIDS.

If the American Catholic church has much to gain from a genuine dialogue with the gay community, it also has much to share with that community. Before gay and lesbian leaders will be able to appreciate fully the wisdom Catholicism has to offer, however, they may need to overcome some stereotypes. Anti-Catholic bigotry has been and still remains part of the cultural scene in the United States, and it is bound to affect the perceptions of many in the gay and lesbian community who are not familiar with the pluriform character of Catholicism. For example, it may come as a surprise to many non-Catholic gay leaders that Cardinal O'Connor does not represent the minds of most Catholics in this country. Moreover, most American Catholics are not dumb sheep who mindlessly follow whatever the pope says. Nor are all clergy and bishops rigid, unfeeling, and out of touch with the experiences of their people. Many priests and bishops have courageously stood up for the gay and lesbian community at great cost to themselves. Gay and lesbian leaders need to be more discriminating as to which Catholics they target, rather than assuming that all Catholics think and feel the same way. The fact that the majority of American Catholic laity have been found consistently to support civil rights for gays and lesbians and for people with AIDS should make it clear that sweeping denunciations of Catholics in the gay press and disturbances of their liturgies are inappropriate. If a fruitful dialogue is to occur, anti-Catholic stereotypes have got to go.

Gay and lesbian activists may also need some "sensitivity training" with regard to the key symbols and values of American Catholics (just as the American bishops may need similar training regarding the symbols and values of the gay community). Ridiculing important Catholic symbols, such as the Mass, the Blessed Virgin, and the crucified Jesus, is not likely to contribute to a climate of dialogue, even when it is done in jest. Just as the American bishops need a greater understanding of and respect for gay symbols and values, so do gays and lesbians need to demonstrate greater respect for the traditional symbols and values of Catholicism.

There are elements of American Catholic thought and practice that could be worthwhile for gay leaders and intellectuals to hear and consider at this time. If I try to sketch out some of these elements, it is not with a view to providing an apologia for the Catholic position, much less to proselytizing. Rather, I believe that a critical look at some elements of Catholic human nature theory can provide some idea of what a more adequate foundation for gay moral and political theory might look like. These elements include: a theory of community that is more adequate to current gay experience than the liberal privatism on which earlier gay thought and politics were understandably but unfortunately founded; a tradition of social justice in which participation in decision making is coming to play a more prominent role; a moral universe in which suffering and death have a meaningful place alongside pleasure and gratification.

The AIDS epidemic has been an occasion for the gay community to outgrow the theories of liberal privatism on which it has relied in the past. This theory grew out of a mid-eighteenth-century interpretation of the work of John Locke[15] and emphasizes individual freedom, unlimited opportunity to pursue material wealth, and severe limitation on government intervention in the lives of individuals. In an earlier period, liberal privatism was found by many gay and lesbian leaders to be both liberating and necessary for survival. In an era when gay men and lesbians could be arbitrarily fired, evicted, arrested, beaten, and even killed, all without legal recourse, the choices for most gay men and lesbians were between being persecuted and being left alone. In such a context, liberal privatism, especially as found in its "do your own thing" version of the 1960s, seemed to be a welcome friend.

But liberal privatism fails to account for much of what we as individuals know to be true: We are intrinsically woven into a social fabric in which we are nourished and give nourishment to others.

For each of us lives in and through an immense movement of the hands of other people. The hands of other people lift us from the womb. The hands of other people grow the food we eat, weave the clothes we wear and build the shelters we inhabit. The hands of other people give pleasure to our bodies in moments of passion and aid and comfort in times of affliction and distress. It is in and through the hands of other people that the commonwealth of nature is appropriated and accommodated to the needs and pleasures of our separate, individual lives, and, at the end, it is the hands of other people that lower us into the earth.[16]

The experiences of gay men and lesbians at the present time are very different from those in the 1960s and 1970s. AIDS has been a moment in which many gay men and lesbians, far from being stereotypically caught up in private, individual pursuits of self-gratification, have demonstrated a tremendous willingness to forgo individual pleasures, contributing vast amounts of time, energy, and money to their community and to the care of those suffering from the disease. The self-fulfillment ethic of the 1960s and 1970s, which idealized gratification of all inner needs and desires, has subsided. With the demise of that ethic has come the rediscovery that an individual's own sense of dignity and freedom can only exist within a context of human solidarity and community and, moreover, one must often forgo the gratification of one's own desires and interests for the good of one's community. In particular, sexual gratification is no longer the only central element in a gay man's identity.[17] While sexual expression remains critical to him, his identity today has more to do with giving compassionate care to dying lovers and friends and a political struggle for just distribution of health care services.

Moreover, political and cultural progress has caused many in the gay and lesbian community to forge a new relationship with the larger American society. Many states have repealed their anti-sodomy statutes, and several municipalities and private corporations have extended medical and other benefits to the partners of gay and lesbian employees. Ordinances at the state and local levels have banned discrimination against gay men and lesbians in housing and employment, and some now recognize gay and lesbian relationships as "domestic partnerships." Anti-hate statutes have likewise been written in many parts of the country to outlaw gay bashing. More and more gay and lesbian couples are becoming legally able to adopt and raise children. Finally, the president of United States, Bill Clinton, told gay men and lesbians during his campaign: "I have a vision of America, and you're part of it." Despite the continuation of hate crimes and bigoted legislation in many places, gay men and lesbians have successfully demanded that they be included within the American picture. It can no longer be said that they are content simply to be left alone. The key word now is inclusion, and inclusion precisely with the unique identity that is theirs as gay men and lesbians.

Liberal privatism no longer adequately reflects the gay and lesbian experience. Indeed, as one gay leader, Benjamin Schatz, has correctly argued, the earlier insistence on the right to privacy now plays into the hands of anti-gay bigots:

Private is, after all, exactly what they [i.e., the anti-gay bigots] want us to be. They don't want us "flaunting" our affection for each other; they don't want us marching on gay pride day, and they certainly don't want open, proud lesbians and gay men taking positions of power. I believe we are fighting less for the right to privacy than for the right not to have to be private.[18]

This emphasis by gay men and lesbians on inclusion has been especially prominent within the AIDS movement. Again and again, AIDS activists, understanding that "Silence = Death," have demanded a voice within the medical and governmental discussions of the epidemic, whether at international AIDS conferences or the National Commission on AIDS. Far from wanting government and the larger society to leave them alone, these AIDS activists have demanded direct government intervention in the epidemic, whether in the form of a national "AIDS czar," more government funds for research and treatment, or new FDA regulations to speed up the release of new drugs. Again, liberal privatism does not adequately account for the current experience and interests of the gay and lesbian community as it confronts the AIDS epidemic. To cite Benjamin Schatz once again, "In the age of AIDS, the right to be left alone seems far less useful and relevant than it used to."[19]

If it is true that liberal privatism no longer serves the gay and lesbian community well, then there is a need to develop other theoretical foundations. It is here that the dialogue with American Catholicism can be helpful.

For in the Catholic worldview, the dignity of the human person is the foundation on which Catholic social theory is built, but that dignity can only be realized in community. In contrast to liberal privatism and individualism, Catholic social theory holds that "being a person means being united with other persons in mutual love." As the American bishops assert, "What the Bible and Christian tradition teach, human wisdom confirms. Centuries before Christ the Greeks and Romans spoke of the human person as a 'social animal' made for friendship, community and public life. These insights show that human beings achieve self-realization not in isolation, but in interaction with others."[20]

Some critics might legitimately fear that such an emphasis on the communal nature of human life opens the door for collective oppression of individuals and minorities who do not fit within the prevailing communal standards. In this case, critics might well charge, collectivism and authoritarianism, the dangers opposite to individualism, arise. Such fears might seem particularly well founded in light of the restoration currently under way in the Catholic church during the present papacy. Nevertheless, Catholic social theory has addressed the dangers of collectivism and authoritarianism by articulating what is known as "the principle of subsidiarity."

This principle, overlooked by many current Vatican administrators, delineates the proper role of government and the larger community vis-à-vis the individual and the smaller group. As originally stated by Pius XI in 1931, subsidiarity means that "that which individual men and women can accomplish by their own initiative and their own industry cannot be taken away from them and assigned to the community; in the same way, that which minor or lesser communities can do should not be assigned to a greater or higher community. To do so is a grave injury and disturbance of the social order; for social activity by its nature should supply help to the members of the social body, never destroy or absorb them."[21]

This principle, then, provides Catholicism's way through the Scylla of an irresponsible individualism on the one side, in which the best government is the least government, and, on the other side, the Charybdis of authoritarian collectivism that oppresses the individual and local groups, subordinating them to the whole. It would imply a government that is neither oppressively interventionist nor irresponsibly passive. For example, the principle of subsidiarity would allow government to play an active role in the fight against AIDS and in advancing civil rights for gay men and lesbians. Yet it would also respect the freedom of individuals and subcultures to act as they deem appropriate. In the words of Catholic sociologist John Coleman, "The law of subsidiary function prescribes that authority act for the common good in accord with the dignity of the human person by allowing men and women and lesser societies through social action to freely pursue their own perfection, diversity, and creativity."[22]

In short, the Catholic theory of human community, as nuanced by the principle of subsidiarity, provides a balanced and more adequate alternative to the liberal privatism on which earlier gay social theory was founded. It more fully accounts for the human need to belong to other human beings. It more adequately speaks to the current need of the gay and lesbian community to be included in the larger cultural and political landscape. It also speaks more effectively to the renewed awareness of the importance of community that has emerged among gay men and lesbians themselves, particularly during the current epidemic. It places an appropriate emphasis on the importance of community in the realization of individual dignity, yet it does so in such a way as to accommodate a genuine diversity and individual freedom. As such, the Catholic theory of human community is worth examination by gay intellectuals and leaders at the present time.

The gay community could also benefit from Catholicism's rich wisdom concerning social justice. That wisdom is organically linked with the Catholic understanding of human community. If it is true that one must be part of a community in order to be fully human, then participation in the life of human community is a fundamental requirement of justice. AIDS activists who have fought long and hard to participate in the deliberations of medical scientists and government policy makers might find these words of the American bishops to be affirming:

> Basic justice demands the establishment of minimum levels of participation in the life of the human community for all persons. The ultimate injustice is for a person or group to be actively treated or passively abandoned as if they were nonmembers of the human race. To treat people this way is effectively to say that they simply do not count as human beings. This can take many forms, all of which can be described as varieties of marginalization or exclusion from social life. . . . These patterns of exclusion are created by free human beings. In this sense they can be called forms of social sin. Acquiescence in them or failure to correct them when it is possible to do so is a sinful dereliction of Christian duty.

> Recent Catholic social thought regards the task of overcoming these patterns of exclusion and powerlessness as a most basic demand of justice. Stated positively, justice demands that social institutions be ordered in a way that guarantees all persons the ability to participate in the economic, political and cultural life of society. The level of participation may legitimately be greater for some persons than for others, but there is a basic level of access that must be made available for all. Such participation is an essential expression of the social nature of human beings and of their communitarian vocation.[23]

Catholic theories of social justice, although frequently disregarded by the church in its own internal practice, nevertheless provide a theoretical and moral framework that those working in this epidemic could find both affirming and politically useful. At a time when gay men and lesbians, especially those with AIDS, are in need of and legitimately demand adequate health care and basic civil rights, the Catholic theory of social justice can provide a moral framework in which to assert such needs and demands.

Finally, gay men and lesbians active in the epidemic could benefit from an understanding of the ways Catholicism has integrated the experience of human suffering and death into its worldview. As we saw earlier, gay culture as we now know it reached a pivotal point during the 1960s when an ethic of self-gratification and pleasure was being asserted. While this new ethic was a welcome corrective to the harsher elements of the Protestant ethic, it was not adequate to the devastation and pain of AIDS that followed a few years later. What is needed is a worldview capable of containing both pleasure and pain, both life and death.

During this time of AIDS, the gay and lesbian worldview must be able to give the experience of sickness and death a meaningful place— must enable its adherents to make some sense out of the suffering and live with it gracefully—if it is to have any credibility. Peter Berger sees such a function as belonging to religion:

> Religion, then, maintains the socially defined reality by legitimating marginal situations in terms of an all-encompassing sacred reality. This permits the individual who goes through these situations to continue to exist in the world of his society—not "as if nothing had happened," which is psychologically difficult in the more extreme marginal situations, but in the "knowledge" that even these events or experiences have a place within a universe that makes sense. It is thus even possible to have "a good death," that is, to die while retaining to the end a meaningful relationship with the nomos of one's society—subjectively meaningful to oneself and objectively meaningful in the minds of others.[24]

Thus, a religious element is crucial to gay culture at this time if a gay worldview is to remain viable in the face of AIDS. A brief mention of one traditionally Catholic understanding of suffering, shared with many other Christians, may illustrate the function religion can play in a time of crisis.

Within the Catholic tradition, the story of Jesus' suffering and death on the cross is a prelude to the story of his resurrection to a fuller life. This "paschal mystery" ascribes to suffering and death a graceful meaning. In Catholic theology, the story of Jesus is a paradigm for all of life itself, and what was true for Jesus is believed to be true for each of us as well: our own experiences of suffering and death lead, by God's grace, to fuller life. Pastoral theologian John J. McNeill states in his reflections on AIDS:

> The essential point is that even death cannot destroy a true, living communion with the living God. The kingdom of the dead does not have the last word in our personal history. Life with God is stronger than death.[25]

Indeed, the paschal mystery and the story of Jesus' death and resurrection serve as the fundamental metaphor—far more fundamental than any scriptural image or story of divine punishment—by which a Catholic understands and gives shape to his or her life.

This story of Jesus can provide a helpful metaphor for one coping with AIDS, for in this story, Jesus, after being ostracized, humiliated, wracked with pain, and finally killed, is raised by God into a fuller and richer life than would otherwise have been possible. In focusing on such a metaphor, a gay man with AIDS is enabled to fully name the pain and rejection that he has likely experienced, yet to see the ways in which that tragedy has opened up a fuller life for him and others. While the Jesus story is likely to have a meaning unique to each individual, it nevertheless seems to ring true for many in the gay community these days who have, in and through the tragedy of AIDS, experienced a deepening compassion, a more profound sense of connection with other people, and a heightened sense of gratitude for life, all as a result of this tragic disease. One can live with AIDS gracefully as a result of this metaphor. Because the story of Jesus seems to account for so many aspects of the contemporary gay and lesbian experience, it seems to me to be an adequate metaphor for gay people to consider at this time.

Moreover, this paschal mystery is not simply an abstract doctrine for Catholics, but rather is embedded in rituals and practices in which each Catholic participates: the Eucharist, the Sacrament of the Sick, and various devotions such as the Stations of the Cross. Such ritual practices allow each participant, with all of his or her experiences of tragedy and loss, to participate in the story of Jesus' death and resurrection, knowing that the sacred canopy remains intact, despite all appearances to the contrary. Within such a world, one can live gracefully, even when in pain.

Such a rich understanding of human suffering is obviously capable of becoming distorted into a cult of suffering in which life and pleasure are stifled and destroyed. As with all metaphors, this metaphor of Jesus' death and resurrection must be used carefully. Nevertheless, the meaning ascribed to suffering by the Catholic tradition, when properly understood, is far more adequate in this time of AIDS than the Dionysian value system of the gay moral universe as it emerged from the 1960s and 1970s. The maturing of gay and lesbian culture will require the development of and respect for a religious element that can serve this necessary function of integrating physical and psychological pain in a healthy and larger worldview. In these days of AIDS, the gay community could benefit from listening to the ways that Catholicism, as well as other traditional religions, have managed to integrate human tragedy without being overcome by it.

AIDS is an occasion for the Catholic and gay/lesbian communities to come together in the hope of alleviating a relentless and tragic suffering. If only for the sake of ending the epidemic, one would hope that the collaboration between these two cultures would continue successfully. Yet even apart from the exigencies of this epidemic, there are many other riches to be gained from this convergence, many other truths to be told by both sides. The hope remains that, within this time of tragedy and loss, the structure of war that has thus far marred the relationship between the gay and Catholic cultures can be turned into the structure of collaboration between fellow citizens who, though unique in their cultural identities and values, can nevertheless speak to each other respectfully.

At the beginning of this book, I described the scene when ACT UP demonstrated at St. Patrick's Cathedral. Another scene now comes to mind as I draw this book to a close.

The devoutly Catholic mother of a young man in his late twenties was devastated to learn that her son was dying of AIDS in San Francisco. Over the years, she had tried to keep in touch with him, but, for reasons she could not fully understand, he had become progressively aloof from her. Now, with the news of his illness, she quickly traveled from her home in the Midwest to see him, perhaps for the last time.

As is frequently the case, the news of her son's diagnosis was the first inkling she had that her son was gay, and this realization compounded her grief and sadness. Upon arriving at his San Francisco home, she was greeted at the door by his lover, whom she had never even heard about. He warmly welcomed her, took her coat, and led her immediately to her son's bedroom.

She stayed several days at the bedside of her son, playing cards and watching television with him, helping with his care, talking to his doctor. But despite her satisfaction in being able to share that time with him, it was obvious that she remained disturbed about her son's homosexuality. This was particularly apparent in the rigidity and coldness with which she responded whenever his lover came into the room.

After a few days, she suggested to her son that it was time to call a priest, and her son agreed. Shortly after arriving at the house, the priest recognized the reason behind the mother's anxiety. After praying with her and her son, he stayed for a chat. He asked her about her life in the Midwest. Eventually he asked her how she had come to meet her husband, now deceased for several years. She began to reminisce about the time they first met, the hat he was wearing, the cafe where they went on their first date. She talked about the bittersweet early years of their marriage, the financial struggles they endured, and the painful fact that her family had not accepted her new husband, feeling that he was somehow beneath them.

As the visit continued, the priest eventually turned to the young man with AIDS. He asked him how he had come to meet his lover. Slowly, the young man began to tell his story of how they met at a party, where they went on their first dates, hiking trips they took, and their decision finally to establish a home together.

As his mother listened to her son, a subtle miracle began to occur. She began to recognize some profound similarities in their two stories. Despite the obvious differences between them, they both seemed to be part of a universe more vast than she had previously imagined. It was not so much that she began consciously to reformulate her ethical construction of her son's homosexuality. Nothing so abstract as all that. Rather, she began to understand that her son had simply but truly fallen in love with another man—just as she had once fallen in love with her husband. How amazing! How wonderful!

Somehow, as she listened to her son speak about his lover, her ethical categories and cultural boundaries, while still intact, seemed much less important. What seemed far more significant was the wonderful and amusing mystery of love and life that could hold both her and her son, each with their own uniqueness.

The AIDS epidemic is a moment when the gay community and the Catholic church come together in the face of immense human pain. We can hope that, without abdicating their respective identities and values, these two cultures can nevertheless find a common ground on which to meet. In this tragic moment, may the structure of war give way to the structure of dialogue. May extravagant compassion be extended, profound truths be shared, rich stories be told, and amazing discoveries be made about the vastness of love and life.

Notes

Introduction

1. Douglas Crimp, *AIDS Demographics* (Seattle: Bay Press, 1990), 131.
2. Quoted in Robert M. Wachter, M.D., *The Fragile Coalition: Scientists, Activists, and AIDS* (New York: St. Martin's Press, 1991), 63.
3. Ibid.
4. Rowland Evans and Robert Novak, "Inside Report: AIDS Education," *San Francisco Examiner*, 31 January 1987, sec. A, p. 7. Also, U.S. Surgeon General and Centers for Disease Control, *Understanding AIDS* (Washington, D.C.: U.S. Department of Health and Human Services, Public Health Service, 1988), HHS Publication No. (CDC) HHS-88-8404.
5. For an instance of Silverman's qualified endorsement of condom education see his "AIDS: The Challenge of a Lifetime," in *AIDS Issues: Confronting the Challenge*, ed. David G. Hallman (New York: Pilgrim Press, 1989), 22.
6. National Conference of Catholic Bishops, "Called to Compassion and Responsibility: A Response to the HIV/AIDS Crisis," *Origins* 19 (30 November 1989): 429.
7. Joshua Gamson, "Rubber Wars: Struggles over the Condom in the United States," *Journal of the History of Sexuality* 1 (October 1990): 262–82.
8. Andrew M. Greeley, *The Catholic Myth: The Behavior and Beliefs of American Catholics* (New York: Charles Scribner's Sons, 1990), 228.
9. Cardinal O'Connor, referring to the work of his own archdiocese, stated at the Vatican's 1989 conference on AIDS that he had "sat with, listened to, emptied the bedpans of, and washed the sores of more than 1,100 persons with AIDS." This work of the New York Archdiocese has been more harshly interpreted by some AIDS activists: "What he meant was that in the hospitals and nursing home facilities the taxpayers pay him to manage through city contracts, he and his minions daily inflict the indignity of their archaic moralism on people dying from a disease he is helping to spread." (Crimp, 133)

Chapter 1

1. Paul Farmer and Arthur Kleinman, "AIDS as Human Suffering," in *Living with AIDS*, ed. Stephen R. Graubard (Cambridge, Mass.: MIT Press, 1990), 357.

2. Robert A. Padgug, "Gay Villain, Gay Hero: Homosexuality and the Social Construction of AIDS," in *Passion and Power: Sexuality in History*, ed. Kathy Peiss and Christina Simmons with Robert A. Padgug (Philadelphia: Temple University Press, 1989), 293.

3. Clifford Geertz, *The Interpretation of Cultures* (New York: Basic Books, Inc., 1973), 46.

4. Charles Rosenberg, "Disease and Social Order in America: Perceptions and Expectations," in *AIDS: The Burdens of History*, ed. Elizabeth Fee and Daniel M. Fox (Berkeley: University of California Press, 1988), 13.

5. Susan Sontag, *AIDS and Its Metaphors* (New York: Farrar, Straus, and Giroux, 1989), 5.

6. Ibid., 14.

7. "Learning to Be a Leper: A Case Study in the Social Construction of Illness," in *Social Contexts of Health, Illness, and Patient Care*, ed. Elliot Mishler (New York: Cambridge University Press, 1981), 169-94.

8. Malcolm Nicolson and Cathleen McLaughlin, "Social Constructionism and Medical Sociology: A Study of the Vascular Theory of Multiple Sclerosis," *Sociology of Health and Illness: A Journal of Medical Sociology* 10 (September 1988): 235.

9. Harold Varmus, the chairman of the Retrovirus Study Group that fashioned the name of the virus, describes the complex political process of naming what we now call the human immunodeficiency virus:

> The forces that influence decisions about them (i.e., the names of viruses) are as various as the forces that influence the naming of a baby, a brook, a bridge, or a city. Scientific principles, political realities, aesthetics, convention, and justice must all be served in the process of finding a species name for a virus. Many questions had to be considered for each suggestion: Is the proposed name consistent with scientific facts and with the tentative classification of the virus? Is there anything objectionable about the name that would prevent its being used? Have those credited with discovery been accorded their right to contribute to the process of naming? Does the name distinguish the virus from those it does not resemble? Is the name really remembered? Is the name likely to create confusion in the future if and when other viruses are isolated? Does the name conform to existing conventions for naming viruses of this general type? ("Naming the AIDS Virus" in *The Meaning of AIDS: Implications for Medical Science, Clinical Practice, and Public Health Policy*, ed. Eric T. Juengst and Barbara A. Koenig [New York: Praeger Publishers, 1989]: 4.)

10. Aaron Wildavsky and Karl Dake, "Theories of Risk Perception: Who Fears What and Why?" *Daedalus* 119 (fall 1990): 54.

11. E. D. Gabay and A. Morrison, "AIDS-phobia, Homophobia, and Locus of Control," paper presented at the annual meeting of the American Psychological Association, Los Angeles, August 1985. Cited in Gregory M. Herek and Eric K. Glunt, "An Epidemic of Stigma: Public Reactions to AIDS," *American Psychologist* 43 (November 1988): 886-91.

12. Peter Conrad and J. Schneiders, *The Medicalization of Deviance: From Badness to Sickness* (St. Louis: C. V. Mosby, 1980), 31.

13. The medicalization of American life conflicts, however, with other traditionally held values. For example, as Talcott Parsons notes, since the sick role bestows exemptions on sick people from ordinary obligations such as work, in the United States we tend to restrict entry into this role and we take steps to ensure that it not become a legitimate lifestyle or culture in its own right. We do this for functional reasons: to keep society working, to keep the economy functioning smoothly.

Thus there is a paradox at work here. On the one hand, traditional values seek to limit people's entry into that sick role. At the same time, medical expansionism seeks to draw more and more members of society into its web. Perhaps the Ehrenreichs are correct in their observation that this paradox works itself out along class lines: The poor are excluded from medical treatment, while the more well-to-do are increasingly medicalized and therapeutocratized. See their "Medicine and Social Control" in *The Cultural Crisis of Modern Medicine*, ed. John Ehrenreich (New York: Monthly Review Press, 1978), 39–79.

14. American Society of Plastic and Reconstructive Surgeons, *Comments on the Proposed Classification of Inflatable Breast Prosthesis and Silicone Gel Filled Prosthesis* (1 July 1989), 4, 5; quoted in Rose Weitz, *Life with AIDS* (New Brunswick, N.J.: Rutgers University Press, 1991), 35.

15. Elliot Friedson, *Profession of Medicine: A Study of the Sociology of Applied Knowledge* (New York: Dodd, Mead, 1974), 206.

16. Allen Brandt, *No Magic Bullet: A Social History of Venereal Disease in the United States* (New York: Oxford University Press, 1987).

17. I agree with Paula Treichler: "Of course, where AIDS is concerned, science can usefully perform its interpretive part: we can learn to live—indeed, *must* learn to live—as though there are such things as viruses. The virus—a constructed scientific object—is also a historical subject, a 'human immunodeficiency virus,' a real source of illness and death that we can apparently—individually and collectively—influence. The trick is to learn to live with this disjunction, but the lesson is imperative." ("AIDS, Homophobia, and Biomedical Discourse: An Epidemic of Signification" in *AIDS: Cultural Analysis, Cultural Activism*, ed. Douglas Crimp [Cambridge, Mass.: MIT Press, 1988], 69.)

18. Activist Michael Lynch, early in the AIDS crisis, cautioned against relinquishing too much authority to medicine:

Another crisis exists within the medical one. It has gone largely unex-
amined, even by the gay press. Like helpless mice we have peremptorily,
almost inexplicably, relinquished the one power we so long fought for in
constructing our modern gay community: the power to determine our
own identity. And to whom have we relinquished it? The very authority
we wrested it from in a struggle that occupied us for more than a hundred
years: the medical profession. (Quoted in Treichler, 40.)

19. Irving Kenneth Zola, "Medicine as an Institution of Social Control," in
The Cultural Crisis of Modern Medicine, ed. John Ehrenreich (New York:
Monthly Review Press, 1978), 84.

20. Farmer and Kleinman, 363f.

21. Farmer and Kleinman, 358–59.

22. Sontag, 24.

23. Mary Douglas, *Purity and Danger: An Analysis of Concepts of Pollution
and Taboo* (London: Ark Paperbacks, 1966), 72.

24. George Lakoff and Mark Johnson, *Metaphors We Live By* (Chicago:
University of Chicago Press, 1980), 148.

25. Jerry Falwell, "AIDS: The Judgment of God," *Liberty Report* 2 (April
1987): 2, 5.

26. Peter Freiberg, "Pat Buchanan's Nasty Nature," *The Advocate* (4
August 1983): 18.

27. Judith Williamson, "Every Virus Tells a Story: The Meaning of HIV
and AIDS," in *Taking Liberties*, ed. Erica Carter and Simon Watney (London:
Serpent's Tail, 1989), 79.

Chapter 2

1. Cindy Patton, "AIDS: Putting the Pieces Together," *Gay Community
News* (24 December 1983), p. 3.

2. See, for example, Robert A. Padgug, "Gay Villain, Gay Hero: Homosexu-
ality and the Social Construction of AIDS," in *Passion and Power: Sexuality in
History*, ed. Kathy Peiss and Christina Simmons with Robert A. Padgug (Phila-
delphia: Temple University Press, 1989), 293–313; Kevin Gordon, "Religion,
Moralizing, and AIDS: A Theological/Pastoral Essay," in *Homosexuality and
Social Justice: Reissue of the Report of the Task Force on Gay/Lesbian Issues,
San Francisco*, new, updated, expanded ed. (San Francisco: The Consultation
on Homosexuality, Social Justice, and Roman Catholic Theology, 1986),
206–37; Philip M. Kayal, " 'Morals,' Medicine, and the AIDS Epidemic,"
Journal of Religion and Health 24 (fall 1985): 218–38.

3. Gordon, 207.

4. Falwell, "AIDS: The Judgment of God," *Liberty Report* 2 (April 1987):
2, 5. Many biblical scholars (e.g., D. S. Bailey in *Homosexuality and the Western Christian Tradition* [Hamden, Conn.: Archon Books, 1975]) have asserted,

contra Falwell, that Sodom was destroyed not because of homosexuality, but because of its gross injustices toward the poor, its inhospitality toward strangers, and, perhaps, for gang rape. Moreover, Mary Douglas would not be surprised to find in Falwell's words an instance in which a fear of physical disease is used to shore up a moral and religious code. See her *Purity and Danger: An Analysis of the Concepts of Pollution and Taboo* (London: ARK Paperbacks, 1989; first published in 1966), 69.

5. Quoted in Gordon, 210.

6. Peter Freiberg, "Pat Buchanan's Nasty Nature," *The Advocate* (4 August 1983): 18ff.

7. As I discuss the relation between the homosexual and AIDS metaphors, I will be focusing primarily on the metaphors for the sexuality of *gay males*. This is not to suggest that other groups (e.g., lesbians, hemophiliacs, ethnic groups) have not been affected by HIV, nor that they have not played a significant role in the American response to the epidemic. I am focusing on the metaphors for gay male sexuality primarily because the first "snapshot" of the HIV crisis in the U.S. portrayed it as a disease of gay men. It was only later on that the threat of HIV to other population groups became apparent.

8. Genesis 2:18.

9. Peter Brown, *The Body and Society: Men, Women, and Sexual Renunciation in Early Christianity* (New York: Columbia University Press, 1988), 21.

10. "Having rigidly subordinated the rational and, therefore, moral use of sex in general to one end—procreation—Aquinas assumes that homosexual acts, since they cannot serve that purpose, must be motivated necessarily and exclusively by a drive toward sexual pleasure." (John J. McNeill, *The Church and the Homosexual*, 3d ed. [Boston: Beacon Press, 1988], 97.)

11. Quoted in McNeill, 93.

12. John Boswell argues from a historical perspective that "the early Christian church does not appear to have opposed homosexual behavior per se. The most influential Christian literature was moot on the issue; no prominent writers seem to have considered homosexual attraction 'unnatural,' and those who objected to physical expression of homosexual feelings generally did so on the basis of consideration unrelated to the teachings of Jesus or his early followers. Hostility to gay people and their sexuality became noticeable in the West during the period of the dissolution of the Roman state—i.e., from the third through the sixth centuries—due to factors which cannot be satisfactorily analyzed, but which probably included the disappearance of urban subcultures, increased governmental regulation of personal morality, and public pressure for asceticism in all sexual matters. Neither Christian society nor Christian theology as a whole evinced or supported any particular hostility to homosexuality, but both reflected and in the end retained positions adopted by some governments and theologians which could be used to derogate homosexual acts." Boswell goes on to point out the variety of homosexual metaphors that have been exploited by saints and scholars over the centuries, including the scriptural stories of David

and Jonathan, Jesus and the beloved disciple, and the stories of early Christian saints. (John Boswell, *Christianity, Social Tolerance, and Homosexuality* [Chicago: University of Chicago Press, 1980], 333.) Many other writers have charged Boswell with giving an overly benign interpretation to the church on this topic, as well as with anachronistically reading a twentieth-century understanding of homosexuality into earlier eras.

13. McNeill, 99.

14. Derrick Sherwin Bailey, *Homosexuality and the Western Christian Tradition* (London: Longmans, Green, 1955), viii.

15. Peter Conrad and J. Schneiders, *The Medicalization of Deviance: From Badness to Sickness* (St. Louis: C. V. Mosby, 1980), 178.

16. Quoted in Conrad and Schneiders, 183.

17. Jeffrey Weeks, *Sexuality and Its Discontents: Meanings, Myths, and Modern Sexualities* (London: Routledge and Kegan Paul, 1986; first published in 1985), 67.

18. Conrad and Schneiders, 182.

19. Weeks, *Discontents*, 67.

20. Ibid., 68.

21. Quoted in Conrad and Schneiders, 184.

22. Weeks, 69.

23. Michel Foucault, *An Introduction,* vol. 1 of *The History of Sexuality,* trans. Robert Hurley (New York: Vintage Books, 1980), 43.

24. Quoted in Weeks, 71.

25. As we will see, this same willingness to argue on scientific grounds would later characterize the 1974 gay rights activists who would make their case to the American Psychiatric Association for declassification of homosexuality as a psychiatric disorder—much to the dismay of medicine's critic Thomas Szaz.

26. Cited in David Greenberg, *The Construction of Homosexuality* (Chicago: University of Chicago Press, 1988), 417.

27. Havelock Ellis, *Psychology of Sex* (London: William Heinemann, 1946; first published 1933), 1.

28. Weeks, 79.

29. M. Schmaus, *Der Glaube der Kirche,* vol. 2 (Munich, 1970), 102, as quoted in Leonardo Boff, *Church: Charism and Power: Liberation Theology and the Institutional Church,* trans. John W. Dierchsmeier (New York: Crossroad, 1986), 142.

30. Thomas M. Thurston, "Homosexuality and Contemporary Roman Catholic Ethical Discussion" (Ph.D. diss., Graduate Theological Union, 1988), 3.

31. Pius XI, *Casti Connubii,* 106, in *Official Catholic Teachings: Love and Sexuality,* ed. Odile M. Liebard (Wilmington, N.C.: McGrath Publishing Company, 1978), 50.

32. Weeks, 128.

33. Quoted in Weeks, 152.

34. Conrad and Schneiders, 187.
35. Quoted in Conrad and Schneiders, 185.
36. Quoted in Conrad and Schneiders, 186.
37. Weeks, 155.
38. Ibid., 148.
39. Irving Bieber et al., *Homosexuality: A Psychoanalytic Study of Male Homosexuals* (New York: Basic Books, 1962).
40. C. W. Socarides, "The Psychoanalytic Theory of Homosexuality, with Special Reference to Therapy," in *Sexual Deviation*, ed. I. Rosen (London: Oxford University Press, 1979), 246.
41. Bieber, 319.
42. C. W. Socarides, *Beyond Sexual Freedom* (New York: Quadrangle Books, 1975), 11.
43. Bieber, 18.
44. Ibid., 264.
45. "It is remarkable, given these assertions, that the data provided by [Bieber's book] *Homosexuality* tend to suggest more modest results. Of the seventy-two patients who were exclusively homosexual at the outset of treatment, 57 percent remained unchanged at the end of the study while 19 percent had become bisexual and only 19 percent exclusively heterosexual. Only by combining the data for those who began treatment as homosexuals and those who began as bisexuals was it possible to state that 27 percent had shifted from homosexuality to exclusive heterosexuality." Socarides, however, claims that more than 50 percent of the strongly motivated homosexuals undergoing his psychoanalytic treatment four or five times a week have become heterosexual. (Ronald Bayer, *Homosexuality and American Psychiatry: The Politics of Diagnosis* [New York: Basic Books, 1981], 33, 38.)
46. Bieber, 319.
47. Bieber, "Homosexuality," in Alfred Freedman and Harold Kaplan, *Comprehensive Textbook of Psychiatry* (Baltimore: Williams and Wilkins, 1967), 973, quoted in Bayer, *Homosexuality in American Psychiatry: The Politics of Diagnosis* (New York: Basic Books, 1981), 34.
48. Bayer, 30–31.
49. Ibid., 35.
50. Jonathan Katz, *Gay American History* (New York: Thomas Y. Crowell, 1976), 132.
51. John D'Emilio, *Sexual Politics, Sexual Communities: The Making of a Homosexual Minority in the United States, 1940–1970* (Chicago: University of Chicago Press, 1983), 21.
52. Thomas Szaz, *Ideology and Insanity* (Garden City, N.Y.: Anchor Books, 1970), 41, as quoted in Bayer, 55. Ironically, Szaz in these words overlooks the fact that "health values" and "moral values" are not so easily separated, and health experts, even in their most technical concerns, are guided, whether consciously or not, by the moral values and symbols of their own cultures.

53. John Coleman, "The Homosexual Revolution and Hermeneutics," in *The Sexual Revolution*, ed. Gregory Baum and John Coleman (Edinburgh: T. and T. Clark Ltd., 1984), 63.

54. D'Emilio, 43.

55. Ibid., 42.

56. Ibid., 65.

57. Quoted in D'Emilio, 81.

58. Quoted in D'Emilio, 81.

59. Quoted in D'Emilio, 117.

60. D'Emilio, 81.

61. Cindy Patton, *Sex and Germs: The Politics of AIDS* (Boston: South End Press, 1985), 125.

62. Clifford Geertz, *The Interpretation of Cultures* (New York: Basic Books, 1973), 127.

63. John D'Emilio and Estelle B. Freedman, *Intimate Matters: A History of Sexuality in America* (New York: Harper and Row, 1988), 327.

64. Franklin Kameny, "Speech to the New York Mattachine Society," July 1964, quoted in D'Emilio, 153.

65. Quoted in D'Emilio, 163.

66. Quoted in D'Emilio, 164.

67. Bayer, 48.

68. In the mid-1960s, the Catholic hierarchy of New York State successfully defeated an attempt by the state legislature to overturn the sodomy law. See D'Emilio, 146.

69. *Pastoral Constitution on the Church in the Modern World* 62, in *Vatican Council II: The Conciliar and Post Conciliar Documents*, 1988 Revised Edition, ed. Austin Flannery, O.P. (Boston: St. Paul Editions, 1988), 967.

70. D'Emilio, 211.

71. Quoted in D'Emilio, 232.

72. Bayer, 186.

73. George Gallup and Jim Castelli, *The American Catholic People: Their Beliefs, Practices, and Values* (Garden City, N.Y.: Doubleday and Company, 1987), 64.

74. "Declaration" 1528, in *Official Catholic Teachings: Love and Sexuality*, ed. Odile M. Liebard (Wilmington, N.C.: McGrath Publishing Company, 1978), 431.

75. "Declaration" 1532, in *Official*, 432.

76. Ibid., 433.

77. As we will see, the advent of the HIV epidemic provoked an identity crisis for those men whose gay identity had been achieved in this period essentially through engaging in the rituals of particular sexual practices that were later deemed unsafe for medical reasons.

78. Bellah and colleagues define "lifestyle enclave" as follows:

A term used in contrast to *community*. A lifestyle enclave is formed by people who share some feature of private life. Members of a lifestyle enclave express their identity through shared patterns of appearance, consumption, and leisure activities, which often serve to differentiate them sharply from those with other lifestyles. They are not interdependent, do not act together politically, and do not share a history. If these things begin to appear, the enclave is on the way to becoming a community. Many of what are called *communities* in America are mixtures of *communities* in our strong sense and *lifestyle enclaves*. (*Habits of the Heart: Individualism and Commitment in American Life* [Berkeley: University of California Press, 1985], 335.)

The assertion I am therefore making in these pages is that the gay community is in fact a community according to Bellah's use of the term, though one that is still in the process of emerging as such.

79. Stephen O. Murray, "Components of Gay Community in San Francisco," in Gilbert Herdt, ed., *Gay Culture in America: Essays from the Field* (Boston: Beacon Press, 1992), 107–46.

80. E. Michael Gorman, "A Special Window: An Anthropological Perspective on Spirituality in Contemporary U.S. Gay Male Culture," in *Constructing Gay Theology*, ed. Michael L. Stemmeler and J. Michael Clark (Las Colinas, Texas: Monument Press, 1991), 49.

81. Robert A. Padgug and Gerald M. Oppenheimer, "Riding the Tiger: AIDS and the Gay Community," in *AIDS: The Making of a Chronic Disease,* ed. Elizabeth Fee and Daniel M. Fox (Berkeley: University of California Press, 1992).

82. Lilliann Kopp, "A Problem of Manipulated Data," in *The Vatican and Homosexuality: Reactions to the "Letter to the Bishops of the Catholic Church on the Pastoral Care of Homosexual Persons,"* ed. Jeannine Gramick and Pat Furey (New York: Crossroad, 1988), 40.

83. Coleman, "The Homosexual Revolution," 62–63.

84. "Letter to the Bishops of the Catholic Church on the Pastoral Care of Homosexual Persons," paragraph 8.

85. "Letter," paragraph 17.

86. "Letter," paragraph 10.

87. John Coleman, "Two Unanswered Questions," in *The Vatican and Homosexuality*, ed. Jeannine Gramick and Pat Furey (New York: Crossroad, 1988), 64.

88. McNeill, *Church and Homosexual*, 232.

89. Archbishop John Quinn of San Francisco has been particularly notable for articulating a softening of the "Letter's" harsher qualities. See his "The AIDS Crisis: A Pastoral Response," *America* 154, no. 24 (June 21–28, 1986), 504–6.

90. A. W. Richard Sipe, in *A Secret World: Sexuality and the Search for Celibacy* (New York: Brunner/Mazel, 1990), states that between 18 and 22 percent of Catholic priests could be regarded as gay. Sipe's estimate, regarded as conservative by some, includes priests involved in homosexual relationships as well as ones who merely have questions about their sexual orientation. See also James G. Wolf, ed., *Gay Priests* (San Francisco: Harper and Row, 1989); R. Wagner, *Gay Catholic Priests: A Study of Cognitive and Affective Dissonance* (San Francisco: Specific Press, 1981); Jeannine Gramick, ed., *Homosexuality in the Priesthood and the Religious Life* (New York: Crossroad, 1989).

91. Edward Shils, *Tradition* (Chicago: University of Chicago Press, 1981), 205.

92. Xavier John Seubert, O.F.M., "The Sacramentality of Metaphors: Reflections on Homosexuality," *Cross Currents* (spring 1991): 62–63.

93. Ibid., 56.

94. "Human Sexuality: Toward a Consistent Ethical Method" (unpublished manuscript), 2–3.

95. Catholic leaders should not repeat the mistake made by some Protestant leaders of simply mirroring the values of whatever social class happens to be on the ascendancy at the time. See Peter Berger's article, "Reflections of an Ecclesiastical Expatriate," in *How My Mind Has Changed*, ed. James M. Wall and David Heim (Grand Rapids, Mich.: Eerdmans, 1991).

Chapter 3

1. Albert R. Jonsen, Foreword to *The Meaning of AIDS: Implications for Medical Science, Clinical Practice, and Public Health Policy*, ed. Eric T. Juengst and Barbara A. Koenig, vol. 1 in *Studies in Health and Human Values* (New York: Praeger Publishers, 1989).

2. Quoted in Richard Goldstein, "The Implicated and the Immune: Responses to AIDS in the Arts and Popular Culture," in *A Disease of Society: Cultural and Institutional Responses to AIDS*, ed. Dorothy Nelkin, David P. Willis, and Scott V. Parris (Cambridge, U.K.: Cambridge University Press, 1991), 36.

3. Jan Zita Grover, "Constitutional Symptoms," in *Taking Liberties: AIDS and Cultural Politics*, ed. Erica Carter and Simon Watney (London: Serpent's Tail, 1989), 153.

4. National Conference of Catholic Bishops, "Called to Compassion and Responsibility: A Response to the HIV/AIDS Crisis" in *Origins* 19, no. 26 (30 November 1989): 423.

5. Ibid., 424.

6. Ibid.

7. Ibid., 425, 428–30.

8. United States Catholic Conference Administrative Board, "The Many Faces of AIDS: A Gospel Response," in *Origins* 17, no. 28 (December 1987): 484.

9. Ibid., 484.
10. "Called," 423.
11. Since the time of the second episcopal statement, several leading scientists, including Dr. Luc Montagnier, who first discovered the human immunodeficiency virus, have begun to have second thoughts about the relation of HIV to AIDS. The discussion is nowhere near resolution. Suffice it to say that it does not appear to be as clear as it once did that HIV alone necessarily causes AIDS.
12. "Called," 423.
13. Ibid., 424.
14. "Faces," 486.
15. "Called," 425.
16. "Faces," 484.
17. "Called," 424.
18. "Faces," 486.
19. "Called," 421.
20. "Faces," 486.
21. Ibid., 487.
22. "Called," 423.
23. Ibid., 423.
24. "Faces," 486–87.
25. "Faces," 487; "Called," 430.
26. "Faces," 485.
27. Ibid., 485.
28. Ibid., 484.
29. Ibid., 487.
30. Ibid., 485.
31. "Called," 424.
32. Ibid., 430.
33. Ibid., 431.
34. Ibid., 428.
35. Ibid., 429.
36. Elizabeth Fee, "Sin Versus Science: Venereal Disease in Twentieth-Century Baltimore," in *AIDS: The Burdens of History*, ed. Elizabeth Fee and Daniel M. Fox (Berkeley: University of California Press, 1988), 121–46.
37. Mary Douglas, *Purity and Danger: An Analysis of Concepts of Pollution and Taboo* (London: ARK Paperbacks, 1989; first published in 1966), 3.
38. "Faces," 486.
39. "Called," 429.
40. James F. Drane, "Condoms, AIDS, and Catholic Ethics," *Commonweal* (22 March 1991): 188.
41. "Faces," 487.
42. Gerald D. Coleman, "Condoms and the Teaching on the Lesser of Two Evils," *Church* (spring 1990): 49.
43. "Faces," 486.

44. Ibid., 488.

45. "Reaction to AIDS Statement, *Origins* 17 (24 December 1987): 490.

46. "Called," 429.

47. The Institute of Medicine of the National Academy of Science argues, for example, "that it is more accurate to speak in terms of 'safer' sex because the unknowns are still such that it would be irresponsible to certify any particular activity as absolutely safe." *Confronting AIDS: Directions for Public Health, Health Care and Research* (Washington, D.C.: National Academy Press, 1986), 97.

48. Joshua Gamson, "Rubber Wars: Struggles over the Condom in the United States," *Journal of the History of Sexuality* 1 (October 1990): 262–82.

49. U.S. Surgeon General and Centers for Disease Control, *Understanding AIDS* (Washington D.C.: U.S. Department of Health and Human Services, Public Health Service, 1988; HHS Publication No. (CDC) HHS-88-8404), 4.

50. In an earlier statement, Bishop Bevilacqua had asserted that "it is not responsible action to use the devastating disease of AIDS as an excuse to promote artificial birth control." "The Questions Raised by School-based Health Clinics," *Origins* 17 (3 September 1987): 188.

51. "Reaction to AIDS Statement," *Origins* 17 (24 December 1987): 490. Catholic ethicist Gerald D. Coleman, who drafted the second statement of the bishops on HIV/AIDS, takes issue with this position:

[I]t is not true, as some suggest, that condoms are "intrinsically evil." Some of the most respected manualists permitted sterility testing when semen was procured in marital intercourse with a perforated condom (for example, Kelly, McCarthy, and Clifford).

This is an important point to make because one can never advocate the use of something that is intrinsically wrong. Such is not the case with a condom. ("Condoms and the Teaching of the Lesser of Two Evils," in *Church* [spring 1990]: 49, 50.)

52. "Called," 429.

53. Ibid., 429.

54. This cultural worldview is not solely that of the official American church. When Pope John Paul II addressed the diplomats at the beginning of his seventh visit to Africa he stated:

The Church is convinced that without *a resurgence of moral responsibility and a reaffirmation of fundamental moral values* any program of prevention based on information alone will be ineffective and even counterproductive. More harmful still are campaigns which implicitly promote—through their lack of moral content and the false security which they offer—the very patterns of behavior which have greatly contributed to the expansion of the disease. ("Promote Human Well-Being," *The Pope Speaks* 36, no. 1 [1990]: 50.)

55. National Conference of Catholic Bishops, "Human Sexuality Document's Birth Control Section," *Origins* 20 (29 November 1990): 404.

56. David Kirp, *Learning by Heart: AIDS and Schoolchildren in America's Communities* (New Brunswick, N.J.: Rutgers University Press, 1989), 26–64.

57. Kirp, 277.

58. Cindy Patton, *Sex and Germs: The Politics of AIDS* (Boston: South End Press, 1985).

59. "The Implicated and the Immune: Responses to AIDS in the Arts and Popular Culture," in *A Disease of Society: Cultural and Institutional Responses to AIDS*, ed. Dorothy Nelkin, David P. Willis, and Scott V. Parris (Cambridge, U.K.: Cambridge University Press, 1991), 39.

60. National Conference of Catholic Bishops, "Economic Justice for All: Catholic Social Teaching and the U.S. Economy," *Origins* 16, no. 3 (5 June 1986): paragraph 63.

61. "Called," 426.

62. "Faces," 483.

63. "Called," 426.

64. Ibid.

65. Ibid.

66. Quoted in "Called," 426.

67. "Called," 430.

68. "Faces," 483.

69. Ibid., 484.

70. "Called," 423.

71. "Faces," 484; "Called," 428.

72. "Called," 424.

73. Ibid., 425.

74. "Faces," 484.

75. Ibid., 485.

76. Ibid.

77. "Called," 430.

78. John Courtney Murray, S.J., *We Hold These Truths: Catholic Reflections on the American Proposition* (Kansas City, Mo.: Sheed and Ward, 1960), 47.

79. "Faces," 484.

80. Ibid.

81. Ibid., 486.

82. Ibid.

83. Ibid.

84. Ibid.

85. Murray, 24.

86. "Reaction to AIDS Statement," *Origins* 17 (24 December 1987): 489.

87. Ibid., 493.

88. In fact, I have the impression that a concerted effort was made on the part of conservative prelates to maintain a distance from the gay community in

the drafting of these documents. An anecdote, reported to me by one of the scholars involved in drafting the bishops' second statement, underscores this impression. Because the variety of episcopal viewpoints seemed so wide, sometimes incoherently so, one of the staff members suggested that an overarching metaphor for the episcopal teaching on AIDS could be the NAMES Project Quilt, a pastiche which nevertheless forms a unity. Cardinal Bernard Law vehemently objected that even to allude to the Quilt would be to legitimize the gay community that had generated it. The staff member's suggestion was roundly rejected.

89. Rose Weitz, *Life with AIDS*, 45–48.

90. Alfred Schutz, "Multiple Realities," in *Collected Papers, Vol. 1: The Problem of Social Reality*, ed. M. Natanson (The Hague: Nijhoff), 207–59, cited in Gregory M. Herek and Eric K. Glunt, "An Epidemic of Stigma: Public Reactions to AIDS," *American Psychologist* 43 (November 1988): 886–91.

91. Susan Sontag, *Illness as Metaphor* (New York: Random House, Vintage, 1979).

92. Gary A. Lloyd, "HIV-Infection, AIDS, and Family Disruption," in *The Global Impact of AIDS*, ed. A. F. Fleming (New York: Alan R. Liss, 1988).

93. George R. Kish, letter to the editor, *America* (7 November 1987): 342.

94. Carol Levine, "AIDS and Changing Concepts of Family," in *A Disease of Society: Cultural and Institutional Responses to AIDS*, ed. Dorothy Nelkin, David P. Willis, and Scott V. Parris (Cambridge, U.K.: Cambridge University Press, 1991), 50.

95. Robert Bellah, *Beyond Belief: Essays on Religion in a Post-Traditional World* (San Francisco: Harper and Row, 1970).

96. Robert Bellah, "The Triumph of Capitalism—or the Rise of Market Totalitarianism?" *New Oxford Review* LVIII (March 1991): 8–15.

97. "Faces," 483.

98. Ibid., 487.

99. Quoted in "Called," 432.

100. "Faces," 483; "Called," 431.

101. "Faces," 487.

102. Ibid.

103. Ibid., 486.

104. Ibid., 484.

105. "Called," 423.

106. Ibid., 431.

107. Xavier John Seubert, "The Sacramentality of Metaphors: Reflections on Homosexuality," in *Cross Currents* (spring 1991): 545.

108. "The Consistent Ethic: An Interview with Joseph Cardinal Bernardin," *Second Opinion: Health, Faith, and Ethics* 8 (July 1988): 111.

109. "Faces," 484.

Chapter 4

1. Quinton Hoare and Geoffrey Nowell Smith, ed. and trans., *Selections from the Prison Notebooks of Antonio Gramsci* (New York: International Publishers, 1971).

2. Special thanks to John Coleman and Robert Bellah for their assistance to me in designing the interview process and instrument I developed for this chapter.

3. These interviews were tape recorded with the permission of the person I was interviewing. I later transcribed these recordings.

4. Albert Hirschman, *Exit, Voice, and Loyalty; Responses to Decline in Firms, Organizations, and States* (Cambridge, Mass.: Harvard University Press, 1970), 83.

5. Andrew M. Greeley, *The American Catholic: A Social Portrait* (New York: Basic Books, 1977), 272.

6. Andrew M. Greeley, *The Catholic Myth: The Behavior and Beliefs of American Catholics* (New York: Scribner's, 1990), 2.

7. This uniquely American style of Catholicism appears to be exemplified more recently in a 1992 Gallup poll reporting that 87 percent (93 percent of those under 35) agreed that the church should permit couples to make their own decisions about birth control; 70 percent (79 percent of those under 35) agreed that Catholics can, in good conscience, vote for political candidates who support legal abortion; 52 percent believed abortion should be legal in many or all circumstances. With regard to gay/lesbian issues, 78 percent said homosexuals should have equal rights in terms of job opportunities, and 46 percent agreed that sexual relationships between gay and lesbian persons in a committed relationship can be morally acceptable. ("Gallup Poll Results Unlikely to Please Vatican," *National Catholic Reporter* 28, no. 33 [3 July 1992]: 6.)

Chapter 5

1. John Courtney Murray, S.J., *We Hold These Truths: Catholic Reflections on the American Proposition* (New York: Sheed and Ward, 1960), 18–19.

2. Murray, 10.

3. USCC Administrative Board, "The Many Faces of AIDS: A Gospel Response," *Origins* 17, no. 28 (24 December 1987): 486.

4. Richard Merleman, *Making Something of Ourselves: On Culture and Politics in the United States* (Los Angeles: University of California Press, 1984), 30.

5. Mary Hunt, "Theological Pornography: From Corporate to Communal Ethics," in *Christianity, Patriarchy, and Abuse*, ed. Joanne Carlson Brown and Carole R. Bohn (New York: Pilgrim Press, 1989), 101.

6. *Rationale for Welcoming the National Dignity Convention to Seattle*, in *Homosexuality and the Magisterium: Documents from the Vatican and U.S.*

Bishops, 1975–1985, ed. John Gallagher (Mt. Rainier, Md.: New Ways Ministry, 1986), 82.

7. Note, for example, that, in their 1991 statement on sexuality, the American bishops relegated to a footnote the Vatican's earlier reference to homosexuality as a disordered inclination. In addition, several bishops throughout the country have either not acted to expel Dignity from church property or have tried to negotiate a compromise that would allow openly gay men and lesbians to continue gathering for liturgies and social events on church property.

8. Robert Bellah et al., *The Good Society* (New York: Alfred A. Knopf), 216.

9. *Justitia in Mundo*, as quoted in Charles E. Curran, "What Catholic Ecclesiology Can Learn from Official Catholic Social Teaching," in *A Democratic Catholic Church: The Reconstruction of Roman Catholicism*, ed. Eugene C. Bianchi and Rosemary Radford Ruether (New York: Crossroad, 1992), 95.

10. Eugene C. Bianchi and Rosemary Radford Ruether, "Conclusion: Toward a Democratic Catholic Church," in *A Democratic Catholic Church: The Reconstruction of Roman Catholicism*, ed. Bianchi and Ruether (New York: Crossroad, 1992), 256.

11. Bianchi and Ruether, 257–58.

12. Not surprisingly, some Catholic pastoral caregivers have produced lapel buttons that read, "The Body of Christ has AIDS."

13. What is true of metaphors in general is likewise true of this Pauline metaphor for the church: It must be used carefully. A misuse of the Body of Christ metaphor would be one that justifies autocratic rule by one or a few who represent the "head," thus leaving the remaining members of the body in a subservient position. Susan Sontag, in *Illness as Metaphor*, has correctly objected to this organic metaphor for this reason. As Ernst Troeltsch once observed, in the church type as represented in Roman Catholicism, "the organic idea of unity is transformed into the idea of authority, which regulates the participation of individuals in the value of the whole in harmony with the infallible authority, without allowing individuals to express an opinion in the matter." (*The Social Teaching of the Christian Churches*, trans. Olive Wyon [New York: The Macmillan Company, 1931], 30.) This linking of organic unity with autocracy is a misuse of Paul's metaphor. Nevertheless, the metaphor, used carefully, represents a genuinely Catholic and valuable instinct for inclusivity and a welcoming of diversity within the church.

14. "Democratie in der Kirche," *Stimmen der Zeit* 182 (July 1968): 1–15, as quoted by Charles E. Curran and Robert E. Hunt, *Dissent In and For the Church* (New York: Sheed and Ward, 1969), 118.

15. This mid-eighteenth-century derivation from Locke, as described by historian John Dunn, secularized Locke's theory, taking it out of the religio-moral context in which Locke had conceived it. Without moral and religious constraints, Locke's theory became distorted, providing the basis for an individualism with rather harsh edges and which he very likely would have rejected.

16. James Stockinger, "Locke and Rousseau: Human Nature, Human Citizenship, and Human Work" (Ph.D. diss., Department of Sociology, University of California, Berkeley, 1990), as quoted in Robert N. Bellah et al., *The Good Society* (New York: Alfred A. Knopf, 1991), 104.

17. Martin P. Levine, "The Life and Death of Gay Clones," in *Gay Culture in America: Essays from the Field*, ed. Gilbert Herdt (Boston: Beacon Press, 1992), 81.

18. Benjamin Schatz, "Should We Rethink the Right to Privacy?" *The Advocate*, no. 571 (26 February 1991): 90.

19. Ibid., 90.

20. National Conference of Catholic Bishops, "Economic Justice for All: Catholic Social Teaching and the U.S. Economy" *Origins* 20 (29 November 1990): paragraph 65.

21. Pius XI, *Quadrigesimo Anno*, no. 23.

22. John Coleman, "Not Democracy, but Democratization," in *A Democratic Catholic Church: The Reconstruction of American Catholicism*, ed. Eugene C. Bianchi and Rosemary Radford Ruether (New York: Crossroad, 1992), 233.

23. "Economic Justice for All," paragraphs 76, 77.

24. Peter Berger, *The Sacred Canopy: Elements of a Sociological Theory of Religion* (New York: Doubleday, 1969), 44.

25. John J. McNeill, *Taking a Chance on God: Liberating Theology for Gays, Lesbians, and Their Lovers, Families, and Friends* (Boston: Beacon Press, 1988), 150.

Bibliography

Bailey, Derrick Sherwin. *Homosexuality and the Western Christian Tradition.* London: Longman's, Green, 1955.

Bayer, Ronald. *Homosexuality and American Psychiatry: The Politics of Diagnosis.* New York: Basic Books, Inc., 1981.

Bellah, Robert. *Beyond Belief: Essays on Religion in a Post-Traditional World.* San Francisco: Harper and Row, 1970.

———. "The Triumph of Capitalism—or the Rise of Market Totalitarianism?" *New Oxford Review* LVIII (March 1991): 8–15.

Bellah, Robert N., Richard Madsen, William M. Sullivan, Ann Swidler, and Steven M. Tipton. *The Good Society.* New York: Alfred A. Knopf, 1991.

———. *Habits of the Heart: Individualism and Commitment in American Life.* Berkeley: University of California Press, 1985.

Berger, Peter. "Reflections of an Ecclesiastical Expatriate." In *How My Mind Has Changed*, ed. James M. Wall and David Heim, 100–112. Grand Rapids, Mich.: William B. Eerdmans, 1991.

———. *The Sacred Canopy: Elements of a Sociological Theory of Religion.* New York: Doubleday, 1969.

Bevilacqua, Bishop. "The Questions Raised by School-based Health Clinics," *Origins* 17 (3 September 1987): 187–88.

Bianchi, Eugene C., and Rosemary Radford Ruether, eds. *A Democratic Catholic Church: The Reconstruction of Roman Catholicism.* New York: Crossroad, 1992.

Bieber, Irving, et al. *Homosexuality: A Psychoanalytic Study of Male Homosexuals.* New York: Basic Books, 1962.

Boff, Leonardo. *Church: Charism and Power: Liberation Theology and the Institutional Church*, trans. John W. Dierchsmeier. New York: Crossroad, 1986.

Boswell, John. *Christianity, Social Tolerance, and Homosexuality.* Chicago: University of Chicago Press, 1980.

Brandt, Allen. *No Magic Bullet: A Social History of Venereal Disease in the United States.* New York: Oxford University Press, 1987.

Brown, Peter. *The Body and Society: Men, Women, and Sexual Renunciation in
    Early Christianity*. New York: Columbia University Press, 1988.
Coleman, Gerald D. "Condoms and the Teaching on the Lesser of Two Evils."
    Church (spring 1990): 49.
Coleman, John. "Not Democracy, but Democratization." In *A Democratic
    Catholic Church: The Reconstruction of Roman Catholicism*, ed. Eugene
    C. Bianchi and Rosemary Radford Ruether, 226–47. New York: Cross-
    road, 1992.
———. "The Homosexual Revolution and Hermeneutics." In *The Sexual
    Revolution*, ed. Gregory Baum and John Coleman. Edinburgh: T. and T.
    Clark Ltd., 1984.
———. "Two Unanswered Questions." In *The Vatican and Homosexuality*,
    ed. Jeannine Gramick and Pat Furey, 59–65. New York: Crossroad, 1988.
Conrad, Peter, and J. Schneiders. *The Medicalization of Deviance: From Bad-
    ness to Sickness*. St. Louis: C. V. Mosby, 1980.
Crimp, Douglas. *AIDS Demographics*. Seattle: Bay Press, 1990.
Curran, Charles E., and Robert E. Hunt. *Dissent In and For the Church*. New
    York: Sheed and Ward, 1969.
Curran, Charles E. "What Catholic Ecclesiology Can Learn from Official Cath-
    olic Social Teaching." In *A Democratic Catholic Church: The Reconstruc-
    tion of Roman Catholicism*, ed. Eugene C. Bianchi and Rosemary Radford
    Ruether, 92–112. New York: Crossroad, 1992.
D'Emilio, John. *Sexual Politics, Sexual Communities: The Making of a Homo-
    sexual Minority in the United States, 1940–1970*. Chicago: University of
    Chicago Press, 1983.
D'Emilio, John, and Estelle B. Freedman. *Intimate Matters: A History of Sexu-
    ality in America*. New York: Harper and Row, 1988.
Douglas, Mary. *Purity and Danger: An Analysis of Concepts of Pollution and
    Taboo*. London: ARK Paperbacks, 1989; first published in 1966.
Drane, James F. "Condoms, AIDS, and Catholic Ethics." *Commonweal* (22
    March 1991).
Ehrenreich, Barbara, and John Ehrenreich. "Medicine and Social Control." In
    The Cultural Crisis of Modern Medicine, ed. John Ehrenreich, 39–79. New
    York: Monthly Review Press, 1978.
Ellis, Havelock. *Psychology of Sex*. London: William Heinemann, 1946.
Evans, Rowland, and Robert Novak. "Inside Report: AIDS Education." *San
    Francisco Examiner*, 31 January 1987, sec. A, p. 7.
Falwell, Jerry. "AIDS: The Judgment of God." *Liberty Report* 2 (April 1987).
Farmer, Paul, and Arthur Kleinman. "AIDS as Human Suffering." In *Living
    with AIDS*, ed. Stephen R. Graubard, 353–78. Cambridge, Mass.: MIT
    Press, 1990.
Fee, Elizabeth. "Sin Versus Science: Venereal Disease in Twentieth-Century
    Baltimore." In *AIDS: The Burdens of History*, ed. Elizabeth Fee and Dan-
    iel M. Fox, 121–46. Berkeley: University of California Press, 1988.

Flannery, Austin, O.P., ed. *Vatican Council II: The Conciliar and Post Conciliar Documents*. Boston: St. Paul Editions, 1988.

Foucault, Michel. *An Introduction*. Vol. 1 of *The History of Sexuality*, trans. Robert Hurley. New York: Vintage Books, 1980.

Freedman, Alfred, and Harold Kaplan. *Comprehensive Textbook of Psychiatry*. Baltimore: Williams and Wilkins, 1967.

Freiberg, Peter. "Pat Buchanan's Nasty Nature." *The Advocate* (4 August 1983): 18.

Friedson, Elliot. *Profession of Medicine: A Study of the Sociology of Applied Knowledge*. New York: Dodd, Mead, 1974.

Gabay, E. D., and A. Morrison. "AIDS-phobia, Homophobia, and Locus of Control," paper presented at the annual meeting of the American Psychological Association, Los Angeles, August 1985. Cited in Gregory M. Herek and Eric K. Glunt, "An Epidemic of Stigma: Public Reactions to AIDS." *American Psychologist* 43 (November 1988): 886–91.

Gallup, George, and Jim Castelli. *The American Catholic People: Their Beliefs, Practices, and Values*. Garden City, N.Y.: Doubleday and Company, Inc., 1987.

Gamson, Joshua. "Rubber Wars: Struggles over the Condom in the United States." *Journal of the History of Sexuality* 1 (October 1990): 262–82.

Geertz, Clifford. *The Interpretation of Cultures*. New York: Basic Books, Inc., 1973.

Goldstein, Richard. "The Implicated and the Immune: Responses to AIDS in the Arts and Popular Culture." In *A Disease of Society: Cultural and Institutional Responses to AIDS*, ed. Dorothy Nelkin, David P. Willis, and Scott V. Parris, 17–42. Cambridge, U.K.: Cambridge University Press, 1991.

Gordon, Kevin. "Religion, Moralizing and AIDS: A Theological/Pastoral Essay." In *Homosexuality and Social Justice: Reissue of the Report of the Task Force on Gay/Lesbian Issues, San Francisco*. San Francisco: The Consultation on Homosexuality, Social Justice, and Roman Catholic Theology, 1986.

Gorman, E. Michael. "A Special Window: An Anthropological Perspective on Spirituality in Contemporary U.S. Gay Male Culture." In *Constructing Gay Theology*, ed. Michael L. Stemmeler and J. Michael Clark (Las Colinas, Tex.: Monument Press, 1991).

Gramick, Jeannine, ed. *Homosexuality in the Priesthood and the Religious Life*. New York: Crossroad, 1989.

Greeley, Andrew. *The American Catholic: A Social Portrait*. New York: Basic Books, Inc., 1977.

———. *The Catholic Myth: The Behavior and Beliefs of American Catholics*. New York: Charles Scribner's Sons, 1990.

Greenberg, David F. *The Construction of Homosexuality*. Chicago: University of Chicago Press, 1988.

Grover, Jan Zita. "Constitutional Symptoms." In *Taking Liberties: AIDS and*

Cultural Politics, ed. Erica Carter and Simon Watney, 147–59. London: Serpent's Tail, 1989.

Hallman, David G., ed. *AIDS Issues: Confronting the Challenge*. New York: Pilgrim Press, 1989.

Herek, Gregory M., and Eric K. Glunt. "An Epidemic of Stigma: Public Reactions to AIDS." *American Psychologist* 43 (November 1988): 886–91.

Hirschman, Albert. *Exit, Voice, and Loyalty; Responses to Decline in Firms, Organizations, and States*. Cambridge, Mass.: Harvard University Press, 1970.

Hoare, Quinton, and Geoffrey Nowell Smith, eds. and trans. *Selections from the Prison Notebooks of Antonio Gramsci*. New York: International Publishers, 1971.

Hunt, Mary. "Theological Pornography: From Corporate to Communal Ethics." In *Christianity, Patriarchy, and Abuse*, eds. Joanne Carlson Brown and Carole R. Bohn. New York: The Pilgrim Press, 1989.

Institute of Medicine of the National Academy of Science. *Confronting AIDS: Directions for Public Health, Health Care and Research*. Washington, D.C.: National Academy Press, 1986.

John Paul II. "Promote Human Well-Being." *The Pope Speaks* 36, no. 1, 1990.

Jonsen, Albert R. Foreword to *The Meaning of AIDS; Implications for Medical Science, Clinical Practice, and Public Health Policy*, ed. Eric T. Juengst and Barbara A. Koenig. Vol. 1 of *Studies in Health and Human Values*. New York: Praeger Publishers, 1989.

Katz, Jonathan. *Gay American History*. New York: Thomas Y. Crowell, 1976.

Kayal, Philip M. " 'Morals,' Medicine, and the AIDS Epidemic." *Journal of Religion and Health* 24 (fall 1985): 218–38.

Kirp, David. *Learning by Heart: AIDS and Schoolchildren in America's Communities*. New Brunswick: Rutgers University Press, 1989.

Kish, George R. Letter to the editor. *America* (7 November 1987): 342.

Kopp, Lilliann. "A Problem of Manipulated Data." In *The Vatican and Homosexuality: Reactions to the "Letter to the Bishops of the Catholic Church on the Pastoral Care of Homosexual Persons,"* ed. Jeannine Gramick and Pat Furey, 40-47. New York: Crossroad, 1988.

Lakoff, George, and Mark Johnson. *Metaphors We Live By*. Chicago: University of Chicago Press, 1980.

Levine, Carol. "AIDS and Changing Concepts of Family." In *A Disease of Society: Cultural and Institutional Responses to AIDS*, ed. Dorothy Nelkin, David P. Willis, and Scott V. Parris, 45–70. Cambridge, U.K.: Cambridge University Press, 1991.

Levine, Martin P. "The Life and Death of Gay Clones." In *Gay Culture in America: Essays from the Field*, ed. Gilbert Herdt. Boston: Beacon Press, 1992.

Liebard, Odile M. *Official Catholic Teachings: Love and Sexuality*. Wilmington, N.C.: McGrath Publishing Company, 1978.

Lloyd, Gary A. "HIV-Infection, AIDS, and Family Disruption." In *The Global Impact of AIDS*, ed. A. F. Fleming. New York: Alan R. Liss, 1988.

McCormick, Richard, S.J. "Human Sexuality: Toward a Consistent Ethical Method." Unpublished manuscript, 1990.

McNeill, John J. *Taking a Chance on God: Liberating Theology for Gays, Lesbians, and Their Lovers, Families, and Friends.* Boston: Beacon Press, 1988.

———. *The Church and the Homosexual.* 3d ed. Boston: Beacon Press, 1988.

Merleman, Richard. *Making Something of Ourselves: On Culture and Politics in the United States.* Los Angeles: University of California Press, 1984.

Murray, John Courtney, S.J. *We Hold These Truths: Catholic Reflections on the American Proposition.* Kansas City, Mo.: Sheed and Ward, 1960.

Murray, Stephen O. "Components of Gay Community in San Francisco." In *Gay Culture in America: Essays from the Field*, ed. Gilbert Herdt, 107–46. Boston: Beacon Press, 1992.

National Conference of Catholic Bishops. "Called to Compassion and Responsibility: A Response to the HIV/AIDS Crisis." *Origins* 19, no. 26 (30 November 1989): 421–36.

———. "Economic Justice for All: Catholic Social Teaching and the U.S. Economy." *Origins* 16, no. 3 (5 June 1986).

———. "Human Sexuality Document's Birth Control Section." *Origins* 20 (29 November 1990): 404.

Nicolson, Malcolm, and Cathleen McLaughlin. "Social Constructionism and Medical Sociology: A Study of the Vascular Theory of Multiple Sclerosis." *Sociology of Health and Illness: A Journal of Medical Sociology* 10 (September 1988).

Padgug, Robert A., and Gerald M. Oppenheimer. "Riding the Tiger: AIDS and the Gay Community." In *AIDS: The Making of a Chronic Disease*, ed. Elizabeth Fee and Daniel M. Fox, 245–78. Berkeley: University of California Press, 1992.

Padgug, Robert A. "Gay Villain, Gay Hero: Homosexuality and the Social Construction of AIDS." In *Passion and Power: Sexuality in History*, ed. Kathy Peiss and Christina Simmons with Robert A. Padgug, 293–313. Philadelphia: Temple University Press, 1989.

Patton, Cindy. "AIDS: Putting the Pieces Together." *Gay Community News*, 24 December 1983, p. 3.

———. *Sex and Germs: The Politics of AIDS.* Boston: South End Press, 1985.

Pius XI. *Casti Connubii.*

———. *Quadrigesimo Anno.*

Quinn, John. "The AIDS Crisis: A Pastoral Response." *America* 154, no. 24 (21–28 June 1986): 504–6.

Rahner, Karl. "Democratie in der Kirche," *Stimmen der Zeit* 182 (July 1968): 1–15.

Rosenberg, Charles. "Disease and Social Order in America: Perceptions and Expectations." In *AIDS: The Burdens of History*, ed. Elizabeth Fee and Daniel M. Fox. Berkeley: University of California Press, 1988.

Sacred Congregation for the Doctrine of the Faith. "Declaration on Certain Questions Concerning Sexual Ethics." In *Official Catholic Teachings: Love and Sexuality*, ed. Odile M. Liebard. Wilmington, N.C.: McGrath Publishing Company, 1978.

Schatz, Benjamin. "Should We Rethink the Right to Privacy?" *The Advocate*, no. 571 (26 February 1991): 90.

Schutz, Alfred. "Multiple Realities." In *Collected Papers, Vol. 1: The Problem of Social Reality*, ed. M. Natanson, 207–59. The Hague: Nijhoff, 1974.

Seubert, Xavier John, O.F.M. "The Sacramentality of Metaphors: Reflections on Homosexuality." *Cross Currents* (spring 1991): 543–66.

Shils, Edward. *Tradition*. Chicago: University of Chicago Press, 1981.

Sipe, A. W. Richard. *A Secret World: Sexuality and the Search for Celibacy*. New York: Brunner/Mazel, 1990.

Socarides, C. W. *Beyond Sexual Freedom*. New York: Quadrangle Books, 1975.

———. "The Psychoanalytic Theory of Homosexuality, with Special Reference to Therapy." In *Sexual Deviation*, ed. I. Rosen, 246. London: Oxford University Press.

Sontag, Susan. *AIDS and Its Metaphors*. New York: Farrar, Straus, and Giroux, 1989.

———. *Illness as Metaphor*. New York: Random House, Vintage, 1979.

Szaz, Thomas. *Ideology and Insanity*. Garden City, N.Y.: Anchor Books, 1970.

Thurston, Thomas. "Homosexuality and Contemporary Roman Catholic Ethical Discussion." Ph.D. diss., Graduate Theological Union, 1988.

Treichler, Paula. "AIDS, Homophobia, and Biomedical Discourse: An Epidemic of Signification." In *AIDS: Cultural Analysis, Cultural Activism*, ed. Douglas Crimp, 31–70. Cambridge, Mass.: MIT Press, 1988.

Troeltsch, Ernst. *The Social Teaching of the Christian Churches*. Trans. Olive Wyon. New York: The Macmillan Company, 1931.

United States Catholic Conference Administrative Board. "The Many Faces of AIDS: A Gospel Response." In *Origins* 17, no. 28 (December 1987): 481–89.

U.S. Surgeon General and Centers for Disease Control. *Understanding AIDS*. Washington, D.C.: U.S. Department of Health and Human Services, Public Health Service, 1988. HHS Publication No. (CDC) HHS-88-8404.

Varmus, Harold. "Naming the AIDS Virus." In *The Meaning of AIDS: Implications for Medical Science, Clinical Practice, and Public Health Policy*, ed. Eric T. Juengst and Barbara A. Koenig. New York: Praeger Publishers, 1989.

Wachter, Robert M., M.D. *The Fragile Coalition: Scientists, Activists, and AIDS*. New York: St. Martin's Press, 1991.

Wagner, R. *Gay Catholic Priests: A Study of Cognitive and Affective Dissonance*. San Francisco: Specific Press, 1981.

Waxler, Nancy. "Learning to Be a Leper: A Case Study in the Social Construction of Illness." In *Social Contexts of Health, Illness, and Patient Care*, ed. Elliot Mishler. New York: Cambridge University Press, 1981.

Weeks, Jeffrey. *Sexuality and Its Discontents: Meanings, Myths, and Modern Sexualities*. London: Routledge and Kegan Paul, 1986.

Weitz, Rose. *Life with AIDS*. New Brunswick, N.J.: Rutgers University Press, 1991.

Wildavsky, Aaron, and Karl Dake. "Theories of Risk Perception: Who Fears What and Why?" *Daedalus* 119 (fall 1990): 41–60.

Williamson, Judith. "Every Virus Tells a Story: The Meaning of HIV and AIDS." In *Taking Liberties*, ed. Erica Carter and Simon Watney, 69–80. London: Serpent's Tail, 1989.

Wolf, James G., ed. *Gay Priests*. San Francisco: Harper and Row, 1989.

Zola, Irving Kenneth. "Medicine as an Institution of Social Control." In *The Cultural Crisis of Modern Medicine*, ed. John Ehrenreich, 80–100. New York: Monthly Review Press, 1978.

Index